Also by Lidia Matticchio Bastianich

Felidia

My American Dream

Lidia's Celebrate Like an Italian

Lidia's Mastering the Art of Italian Cuisine

Lidia's Egg-citing Farm Adventure

Lidia's Commonsense Italian Cooking

Lidia's Family Kitchen: Nonna's Birthday Surprise

Lidia's Favorite Recipes

Lidia's Italy in America

Nonna Tell Me a Story: Lidia's Christmas Kitchen

Lidia Cooks from the Heart of Italy

Lidia's Italy

Lidia's Family Table

Lidia's Italian-American Kitchen

Lidia's Italian Table

La Cucina di Lidia

LIDIA'S

a Pot, a Pan, and a Bowl

LIDIA'S
a Pot, a Pan, and a Bowl

Simple Recipes for Perfect Meals

Lidia Matticchio Bastianich
and Tanya Bastianich Manuali

Photographs by Armando Rafael

ALFRED A. KNOPF

NEW YORK 2021

THIS IS A BORZOI BOOK
PUBLISHED BY ALFRED A. KNOPF

www.aaknopf.com

Knopf, Borzoi Books, and the colophon are registered
trademarks of Penguin Random House LLC.

Library of Congress Cataloging-in-Publication Data
Names: Bastianich, Lidia, author. | Manuali, Tanya Bastianich,
author. | Rafael, Armando, photographer.
Title: Lidia's a pot, a pan, and a bowl: simple recipes
for perfect meals / Lidia Matticchio Bastianich and
Tanya Bastianich Manuali; photographs by Armando Rafael.
Other titles: A pot, a pan, and a bowl
Description: New York: Alfred A. Knopf, 2021. | Includes index.
Identifiers: LCCN 2020050353 (print) | LCCN 2020050354 (ebook) |
ISBN 9780525657408 (hardcover) | ISBN 9780525657415 (ebook)
Subjects: LCSH: One-dish meals. | LCGFT: Cookbooks.
Classification: LCC TX714 .B376 2021 (print) | LCC TX714 (ebook) |
DDC 641.82—dc23

LC record available at https://lccn.loc.gov/2020050353
LC ebook record available at https://lccn.loc.gov/2020050354

Interior photography by Armando Rafael
Jacket design by Kelly Blair

Manufactured in Canada

First Edition

I dedicate this book and extend my heartfelt gratitude to all of the first responders who head to the front lines every day to protect each and every one of us. I would like to thank them for their dedication, commitment, and courage, especially in 2020. I nurture, give, share, and express love through cooking, preparing, and ultimately sharing food, because it is what I know best. The recipes in this book are simple and straightforward and delicious for all of us to cook and share with our family, our friends, people in need, and people who deserve our gratitude, like the first responders.

First responders, you are a special breed,
and my pot is always on the stove for you.
Grazie.

Contents

Acknowledgments

There are many people to thank for pulling a cookbook together; it is a project that requires talented people, and, having written thirteen cookbooks, Tanya and I could not do it alone. It is essential that the team be in the same state of mind about what we want to convey to the reader, the cook, and how to convey it in the simplest and most inviting way, so the home cook will want to take the book into the kitchen and cook. To achieve all of this, we need foolproof recipes—enticing, simple, photogenic recipes that tell a story. The cook needs to feel confident that he or she will succeed with the recipes. Then there is the whole visual aspect of designing a book, a book that stands out on the shelf, a book that beckons shoppers to take it in their hands and have a look. Preparing a cookbook takes about two years from start to finish, so here is the extraordinary team that makes it all happen. Grazie to all of you.

Amy Stevenson has been testing recipes and heading my Public Television show kitchen for many years, and she was with us testing each of the recipes in this book, keeping me in line. Sharon Douglas, you worked hard and steadily in the kitchen, and I really appreciate that. I thank Peter Gethers and Tom Pold: it was a pleasure working on the book with both of you! I send a heartfelt thank-you to Paul Bogaards for years of friendship and support and for always being enthusiastic about our books. You are a believer, and we love that. To our Knopf promotional mavens, Sara Eagle and Sarah New, we are so thankful for your work in promoting the book. Thank you, Kristen Bearse, Kelly Blair, and Anna Knighton, for designing it—inside and out—and making it all look so good. It is a tough job to pull it all together, and thank goodness we have you to do it for us. Armando Rafael, it was simply a pleasure. Your work in photography is extraordinary, and you are an absolute pleasure to work with. Your keen eye captured all the beauty and feeling of my food. Biagio Dell'Aiera, wonderful to have you with us during photography. I appreciate your professionalism and sense of humor.

Thank you to the American Public Television team for the fabulous work done in the distribution of my public television series and to Laurie Donnelly, Salme Lopez, Bara Levin, and Matthew Midura at WGBH. Our years together have been great ones. I would also like to thank the many underwriters of my series who help me to continue sharing recipes with my fans and restaurant customers: Cento, Consorzio del Grana Padano, Rovagnati Gran Biscotto, Auricchio Provolone, Locatelli Pecorino Romano, Fabbri, and Olitalia. Thank you, too, to the wonderful showroom consultants at Clarke, who provide the gorgeous kitchen in which the show is filmed.

I must also thank the Tavola Productions team for their efficient work on the companion twenty-six-part public television series. There are many of you, but I must give a shout-out to Shelly Burgess Nicotra, Erika Heymann, Nicole Morgan, Brittany Turke, Hayden 5, Amy Stevenson, Michelli Knauer, and their teams for their ability to pull the series together during the pandemic. I also want to thank Merilay Fernandez and Beagleshark for amazing post-production work.

And of course we always include family: thank you, Olivia, Lorenzo, Miles, Ethan, and Julia for the great tasters that you are.

The years 2020/2021 have hard for all of us. But for me it has been especially hard losing my dear mother. Grandma Erminia, who you all loved, turned 100 in January 2021 and passed in February 2021. I could not ask for more; we lived life together for quite a few years. Nonetheless, it is hard not having her around to share memories and recipes, give me advice, and be my official taster and critic. For me, she still resonates in every recipe, aroma, and flavor in our kitchen.

Introduction

Sometimes, you just want to cook something that doesn't leave you with a pile of dishes. That's why one-or-two-pot, -pan, or -bowl cooking just makes sense to me. Whether they require a Dutch oven, a sheet pan, or a pot for pasta, these dishes are no-brainers. Some people think of "one-pot cooking" as a term that applies only to dishes cooked in a single vessel, but I take a more expansive view: you may need an extra bowl or plate along the way. But rest assured, the recipes in this book are some of my absolute favorites, streamlined to be as straightforward to cook as possible, using a minimal number of pots and pans, without sacrificing any flavor. These are classic Italian dishes, like Summer Tomato and Basil Risotto with Mozzarella (page 89), Balsamic Chicken Stir-Fry (page 159), Matalotta-Style Mixed Fish Stew (page 125), Skillet Gratinate of Chicken, Mushrooms, and Tomato (page 140), and Skillet Gratinate of Pork, Eggplant, and Zucchini (page 143), adapted for fuss-free cooking.

For me as a chef, creating simple, minimally messy dishes is a creative challenge I enjoy. I feel like a composer, composing a symphony; cooking this way affords me a wonderful opportunity to think about layering flavors. I begin by choosing ingredients that I think will harmonize when cooked together. Then I also need to think about timing—the most important element of cooking with just one pot, pan, or bowl—and when to add each ingredient. How long should the ingredients cook together? How will the textures of each contribute to the dish at the finish?

In many ways, making a one-or-two-pot meal is cooking at its basic level, but also at its most diverse. Some dishes take time—like soups, braising tougher cuts of meat, or cooking root vegetables—but there are many quick one-pot dishes that are just as delicious and that can be prepared much faster. These recipes also tend to be balanced, incorporating vegetables, legumes, and meat, making the meal healthier. And, of course, it is convenient—there's much less to wash up!

The recipes in this book are simple but delicious, and almost all of them can be served either as a one-course meal, or as part of a multicourse affair.

Take, for example, the chapter of egg recipes. Each one of those dishes, when paired with a tossed green salad, would make for a delicious brunch, especially the Sweet Potato and Ham Frittata (page 8) and Spinach, Bread, and Ricotta Frittata (page 9), or the Spinach and Fontina Casserole (page 18). Or stuff a toasted hero with one of the frittatas and you have a great picnic or a meal for a day at the beach with the kids.

In the salad chapter, you'll find many recipes that can double as an appetizer, like the "Antipasto" Rice Salad (page 55); Shaved Artichoke, Spinach, and Mortadella Salad (page 61); or Crab and Celery Root Salad (page 64). A salad like Summer Panzanella (page 59) or Winter Panzanella (page 60) can serve as a side dish to grilled or roasted meats, like London Broil with Peppers and Onion (page 152) or Skillet Ricotta Mini–Meat Loaves (page 145); or fish dishes like the Mixed Seafood Bake (page 117). Certainly, most of these salads can be turned into main dishes, just by increasing the portion sizes.

Pasta and rice dishes—or *primi*, as they are called in Italy—can be the center of the meal all by themselves, like the Skillet Lasagna (page 86), No-Boil Stuffed Shells (page 88), or Mushroom and Sausage Risotto (page 90), or, for a warm-weather version, perhaps a summer meal by the pool, I like the Mezzi Rigatoni with Raw Tomato Sauce (page 83). Pasta as a *primo* can be just that, a first course or an appetizer. In Italy, two or three forkfuls of pasta before a main course is quite customary.

When it comes to the fish and meat recipes, remember you can make these dishes even more substantial by adding beans, like in Monkfish Brodetto with Cannellini (page 111) and Halibut with Saffron Fregola (page 120). Recipes like Skillet Chicken Thighs with Cerignola

Olives and Potatoes (page 135), Chicken Cacciatore (page 138), and Skillet Sausages with Fennel and Apples (page 147) are a meal in themselves. You might also consider serving some of the fish dishes shared as an appetizer when you are planning a two-course meal—for example, the Seared Tuna with Balsamic Onions and Arugula-and-Fennel Salad (page 108), or Grilled Calamari Salad (page 116).

All of which is to say that one-pot, one-pan, and one-bowl meals are just as substantial—and just as varied—as those cooked with a whole kitchen's worth of cooking vessels. These recipes are perfect for a weeknight dinner with your family, but for more elaborate occasions, such as when you have guests, I like to enhance them with a good selection of breads to begin, from buttery brioche, crunchy baguettes, and semolina bread to deep and dark pumpernickel or twelve-grain breads. The addition of grissini, taralli, or crostini always embellishes a bread basket. At either the beginning or the end of a meal, a board of cheeses, such as Taleggio, Toma, Caprino, Gorgonzola, or Grana Padano with some delicious Mostarda (page 175) is always welcome. Especially if you add some ripe seasonal fruit and some toasted almonds and hazelnuts. And, of course, some good Italian cookies and an espresso at the end of a meal never fail to draw applause for the chef.

Finally, it is impossible to talk about one-pot cooking—or any kind of low-fuss cooking—without mentioning the Instant Pot. The electric pressure cooker is a relatively new piece of kitchen equipment that many home cooks have fallen in love with. It's certainly a time saver, and I'm often asked how my recipes will translate when it's used. Many of the dishes in this book will work well—especially Vegetable Soup with Poached Eggs (page 15); Lentil and Pasta Soup (page 24); Stracciatella with Chicken and Vegetables (page 25); Turkey, Mushroom, Chestnut, and Barley Soup (page 28); Shrimp, Swiss Chard, and Potato Chowder (page 39); Poached Chicken and Giardiniera Salad (page 46); Boiled Beef Salad (page 66); Chicken and Rice (page 96); Poached Chicken and Vegetables in Broth with Green Sauce (page 136); Chicken Cacciatore (page 138); Lamb and Winter Squash Stew (page 151); Beer-Braised Beef Short Ribs (page 154); and Pork Guazzetto with Beans (page 158). You just need to be willing to experiment—and to remember a few things:

- Since I like to cook with leftovers in mind, the largest electric pressure cooker, about an eight-quart size, is best for preparing my recipes.
- Braises are wonderful in the pressure cooker, because it takes the fattier cuts of meat and cooks them under pressure until they are tender and flavorful, in half the time (or less!) of a stovetop or oven braise. Some soups will work well also, though many of my soup recipes will have to be scaled down to fit, and you will need to use less liquid (see the next point), since there is no evaporation. Beans are also wonderful in the electric pressure cooker: they turn out very silky in a short amount of time.
- When adapting one of my recipes, remember not to fill the pot more than two-thirds full. Since you are cooking with the lid on and under pressure, you will need less liquid to begin with. I'd start with half the liquid called for in the recipe as a rule of thumb, but you do need at least a cup of liquid to get to pressure reliably. If using the pressure cooker's natural release, cut the cooking time of the recipe by 15 minutes since food will continue to cook.
- Most of my recipes will work just fine when adapted for the electric pressure cooker. Just leave the pressure switch in the sealed position, as this lets the pressure release slowly. When the pressure is fully released the lid will unlock and open, using natural release, so you don't need to worry about overcooking.
- Many of my braise recipes require adding ingredients in stages, starting with the proteins and harder vegetables and adding the quicker-cooking ones later on. You can still do this in the electric pressure cooker. You can cook the protein till it's almost ready, release the pressure, add the quicker-cooking ingredients, and return it to pressure for a short time, or you can just bring the liquid to a simmer, uncovered, on the "sauté" setting and finish that way.
- If your finished dish is more watery than you would like, you can also reduce the cooking juices down on the high "sauté" setting. You can also bring it to a simmer and add a tablespoon or two of flour mixed with enough water so you can drizzle it into the pot, though make sure to simmer it for a few minutes to remove the raw flour taste.

- For dishes with dairy elements—for example, grated cheese—always add them at the end, just as I do in my regular recipes.

One important thing to remember about one-pot and -pan cooking is not to fret about what you will cook in or about whether you have the right vessel or not. Something you already have at home will most likely work. Read the instructions on the cooking vessel recommended in the recipe, and choose something as close as possible to what is recommended.

Whether you are cooking in an Instant Pot or a Dutch oven, or on a baking sheet; for dinner with your kids on a Tuesday or a party with friends—always keep cooking fun, welcoming, and delicious, and an expression of your love and affection for the people around your table.

LIDIA'S

a Pot, a Pan, and a Bowl

EGGS

Scrambled Eggs with Asparagus and Scallions 7
Uova Strapazzate con Asparagi e Scalogno

Sweet Potato and Ham Frittata 8
Frittata di Patate Dolci e Prosciutto Cotto

Spinach, Bread, and Ricotta Frittata 9
Frittata di Spinaci, Pane, e Ricotta

Fried Potatoes with Sausage and Eggs 10
Frittata di Salsicce e Patate

Baked Eggs and Potatoes 11
Uova e Patate al Forno

Eggs Poached in Spicy Tomato Sauce with Eggplant 13
Uova in Purgatorio con Melanzane

Boiled Dandelion Greens, Tuna, and Egg Salad 14
Insalata di Cicoria, Tonno, e Uova Sode

Vegetable Soup with Poached Eggs 15
Zuppa di Verdura con Uova in Camicia

Breakfast Risotto 16
Risotto di Colazione

Cauliflower and Butternut Squash Hash 17
Pasticcio di Cavolfiori e Zucca

Spinach and Fontina Casserole 18
Spinaci e Fontina in Casseruola

Eggs are the perfect food. Accessible, easy to prepare, and versatile, they fit well on the menu of every meal: breakfast, brunch, lunch, or dinner. And, most of the time, cooking them requires only one pot. The first thing I recall ever cooking was a scrambled egg, with my maternal grandmother. Chickens are ever present in every Italian courtyard, and so she always had a few dozen running around. As a young girl, I was the designated egg-collector every morning. I had a little basket lined with hay, and off I went. The easy pickings were the nests where the chickens had laid an egg and left, but some chickens would go and lay their egg in a nest where there was already an egg. Those chickens would usually protest when I went under them with my hand to look for the eggs, and sometimes they would peck me. But I was happy when my basket was filled with eggs, because I knew that that day maybe a frittata with wild asparagus, or some homemade pasta, or a dessert would be on the table. And when Grandma had more eggs than she could use, she would sell them to the neighbors or at the market.

If you are not fortunate enough to have your own chickens, as I did then, it is best to buy eggs from a small farmer with free-range chickens in the fields. But, short of that, look for organic eggs from pasture-raised chickens that have had a chance to roam free. The yolk of these eggs will reflect the food the chickens ate: they'll be bright yellow and have more nutritional value and flavor. On the other hand, the color of the shell, brown or white, is simply an indication of the species of chicken that laid the egg. Eggs come in different sizes, but I would suggest buying large ones, since most of the recipes in this book call for them.

To determine the freshness of your eggs, crack one on a flat plate. If the white part, the albumen, is tight around the egg yolk and the egg yolk stands out, it is a sign that the egg is fresh. If the albumen runs off on the plate, away from the yolk, and the egg yolk lies flat on the plate, the egg is still good but less fresh.

To store eggs, it is best to leave them in the container they came in from the market and check that the pointed end is down and the rounded end is up: this assures that the air pocket in the egg is also up, which keeps the egg fresh longer. When eggs are put up for sale, they are washed at the farm with antibacterial soap, which removes not only bacteria but the egg's natural protective oils as well. Eggs can last up to four or five weeks in the refrigerator, but you can extend their life span up to four months if you wash them with antibacterial soap, dry them, and then coat them with mineral oil, which you can buy at your pharmacy. You can freeze eggs as well, but not in their shells: you need to crack them and whisk them, then freeze them in appropriate plastic containers, one or two eggs in each. Frozen eggs will last about a year. When you're ready to use them, defrost and proceed.

Scrambled Eggs with Asparagus and Scallions

Uova Strapazzate con Asparagi e Scalogno

SERVES 4 • Use medium-thickness asparagus here—they're substantial enough that they won't become mushy, but tender enough that they can cook in the skillet without your having to add liquid. To prep the asparagus, break the woody bottoms at the base of the stalk (they'll break naturally). Peel the lower third of the stalks, and cut as directed below. I like the eggs here to be soft and somewhat runny.

Active Time: 20 minutes

Total Time: 20 minutes

3 tablespoons extra-virgin olive oil

1 bunch medium-thickness asparagus, tough stems trimmed, stalks cut into 1-inch pieces

Kosher salt

Peperoncino flakes

4 scallions, chopped, including green parts

8 large eggs

½ cup milk

1 cup finely diced sharp cheddar or mild provolone

4 thick slices country bread, toasted

Heat the olive oil in a large nonstick skillet over medium heat. Add the asparagus, and season with salt and a large pinch of peperoncino. Toss to coat in the oil. Cover, and cook over medium heat until the asparagus are crisp-tender, 4 to 5 minutes.

Uncover, add the scallions, and toss to combine. Cook until the scallions are wilted and bright green, about 2 minutes.

Meanwhile, whisk the eggs in a large bowl with the milk. Season with ½ teaspoon salt. Pour the eggs over the asparagus and scallions, and sprinkle with the cheese. Cook, stirring with a rubber spatula, until the eggs are scrambled to your liking, 3 to 4 minutes for softly scrambled eggs. Serve over the toasted bread.

Sweet Potato and Ham Frittata

Frittata di Patate Dolci e Prosciutto Cotto

SERVES 6 TO 8 • You could also make this frittata with a large peeled Idaho potato, but I like the subtle sweetness the sweet potato adds to the mix. Add the eggs to the hot pan, give it a minute or two, then lower the heat to medium and move the pan around on the burner to get a nice crust all over the bottom of the frittata before putting it in the oven to bake.

Active Time: 30 minutes

Total Time: 45 minutes

3 tablespoons extra-virgin olive oil

One 8-ounce sweet potato, peeled and sliced into ¼-inch-thick half-moons

8 ounces thickly sliced prosciutto cotto, diced

1½ bunches scallions, chopped, including green parts (about 2 loosely packed cups)

Kosher salt

Freshly ground black pepper

10 large eggs

½ cup freshly grated Grana Padano

Preheat the oven to 375 degrees. Heat a 10-inch nonstick skillet over medium heat. Add the olive oil. When the oil is hot, add the sweet potatoes and toss to coat them in the oil. Once the sweet potatoes begin to brown, add ¼ cup water, and simmer until they begin to soften, about 8 minutes. Increase the heat to reduce away the water.

Add the prosciutto cotto, and cook until it's brown and crisped, about 3 minutes. Add the scallions, and cook until they're wilted, about 2 minutes. Season with salt and pepper.

Meanwhile, whisk the eggs and Grana Padano in a large bowl with ½ teaspoon salt, and season with pepper. Smooth the vegetables into an even layer in the skillet, and pour the egg mixture over them. Lower the heat to medium low, and cook to give the frittata a nice crust, 3 to 4 minutes. Bake in the oven until the frittata is set all the way through, 12 to 15 minutes. Let it cool in the pan for 5 minutes before sliding it out and cutting it into wedges to serve.

Spinach, Bread, and Ricotta Frittata

Frittata di Spinaci, Pane, e Ricotta

SERVES 4 TO 6 • This dish is a cross between a frittata and a bread pudding. You can use just about any bread you like here, as long as it is not too dense. It is especially tasty with day-old focaccia or brioche cubes.

Active Time: 30 minutes

Total Time: 50 minutes

3 tablespoons extra-virgin olive oil

3 leeks, white and light-green parts, halved lengthwise and sliced ½ inch thick

1 bunch spinach, stemmed and coarsely chopped (about 4 cups)

8 large eggs

½ cup milk

Kosher salt

Freshly ground black pepper

2 cups ½-inch crustless country-bread cubes

¼ cup freshly grated Grana Padano

1 ripe medium tomato, thinly sliced

1 cup fresh ricotta

Preheat the oven to 375 degrees. Add the olive oil to a 10-inch nonstick skillet over medium heat. When the oil is hot, add the leeks, and cook until they begin to soften, 3 to 4 minutes. Add the spinach; then cook and stir until it's wilted, 5 to 7 minutes. Increase the heat, and cook away any moisture in the pan.

Meanwhile, whisk the eggs in a large bowl with the milk, 1 teaspoon salt, and several grinds of pepper. Add the bread cubes and grated cheese, and let soak until the bread is moistened, 5 minutes. Pour the egg-and-bread mixture into the skillet. Cook until the sides begin to set, 2 to 3 minutes. Set the sliced tomatoes on top of the egg mixture. Dollop the ricotta in the spaces between the tomato slices. Set the pan in the oven to bake until the frittata is set all the way through, 15 to 18 minutes. Let it cool in the pan for 5 minutes before sliding it out and cutting it into wedges to serve.

Fried Potatoes with Sausage and Eggs

Frittata di Salsicce e Patate

SERVES 6 • If you'd like to make this dish vegetarian, omit the sausage and up the vegetables. You could also add diced zucchini or eggplant along with the peppers. If you have leftover boiled or baked potatoes on hand, use those, and shorten the initial cooking time for the potatoes. To facilitate the addition of the eggs, crack each of them into separate espresso cups before adding.

Active Time: 30 minutes

Total Time: 30 minutes

3 tablespoons extra-virgin olive oil

1¼ pounds small russet potatoes, peeled, halved, and thinly sliced into half-moons

Kosher salt

8 ounces sweet Italian sausage, removed from casings

1 small onion, sliced

1 red bell pepper, sliced

Peperoncino flakes

6 large eggs

2 tablespoons chopped fresh Italian parsley

Heat the olive oil in a 12-inch skillet over medium heat. Scatter in the sliced potatoes, and season with ½ teaspoon salt. Cook, tossing in the oil, until the potatoes begin to brown, about 5 minutes. Crumble the sausage into the pan in large chunks. Cook and stir until the sausage begins to brown, 2 to 3 minutes. Add the onion and bell pepper, and toss well. Season with a little salt and peperoncino, cover, and cook, stirring occasionally, until the vegetables are golden and tender, 10 to 15 minutes.

Uncover, and make six indentations in the potato mixture with the back of a tablespoon. Break the eggs into the indentations, and season them with salt. Cover, and cook over medium heat until the eggs are set to your liking, 6 to 7 minutes for set whites with still-runny yolks. Sprinkle with parsley and serve. Cook longer if you like your eggs not so runny.

Baked Eggs and Potatoes

Uova e Patate al Forno

SERVES 4 • This is a crowd pleaser and an excellent brunch dish. Just make sure the vegetables are cooked before you add the eggs. It is a recipe that you can multiply easily when you suspect you might have a few extra guests. It also makes an excellent vegetarian dish if you substitute some sliced zucchini or other vegetables for the ham or prosciutto.

Active Time: 25 minutes

Total Time: 40 minutes

2 medium russet potatoes (about 1 pound)

2 tablespoons unsalted butter, plus melted butter for brushing the ramekins

4 scallions, chopped

2 ounces thickly sliced prosciutto cotto or other cooked ham, chopped

Kosher salt

Freshly ground black pepper

1 cup heavy cream

4 large eggs

2 tablespoons panko bread crumbs

2 tablespoons freshly grated Grana Padano

2 tablespoons chopped fresh Italian parsley

Toasted bread, for serving

Preheat the oven to 375 degrees. Prick the potatoes all over with a fork. Place them on a microwave-safe plate and microwave for 5 minutes. Flip the potatoes, and microwave until they're tender when poked with a knife, 3 to 5 minutes, depending on the strength of your microwave. Cool slightly; then peel and cut into chunks. Brush four individual gratin dishes with melted butter.

Heat a large skillet over medium heat. Add the 2 tablespoons butter. When it's melted, add the potatoes, and cook until they're browned and crisp, 3 to 4 minutes. Add the scallions and ham, and cook until the ham begins to crisp, about 2 minutes. Season with salt and pepper. Divide the mixture among the ramekins. Pour ¼ cup cream into each ramekin. Break an egg on top, and sprinkle with ground pepper. Toss together the panko and grated cheese in a small bowl. Sprinkle over each ramekin. Set the ramekins on a baking sheet for easy transportation in and out of the oven.

Bake until the eggs are set to your liking, 10 to 15 minutes for set whites with slightly runny yolks. Sprinkle with chopped parsley, and serve with toasted bread.

Eggs Poached in Spicy Tomato Sauce with Eggplant

Uova in Purgatorio con Melanzane

SERVES 4 · To make sure all of the yolks stay intact, I like to break each egg individually into a ramekin before slipping it into the sauce. If you wet the inside of the ramekin with water before breaking the egg in, it will slide out more easily. This is a great brunch dish, and you can prepare the sauce in advance. Then, when your guests arrive, bring it back to boiling and add the eggs.

Active Time: 20 minutes

Total Time: 20 minutes

¼ cup extra-virgin olive oil

1 medium Italian eggplant, peeled and cubed

1 medium onion, chopped

3 tablespoons drained capers in brine

¼ cup pitted oil-cured black olives, halved

Kosher salt

Peperoncino flakes

One 28-ounce can whole San Marzano tomatoes, crushed by hand

½ teaspoon dried oregano, preferably Sicilian oregano on the branch

8 large eggs

¼ cup chopped fresh basil (optional)

Wedge of pecorino, for grating (optional)

Heat the oil in a large nonstick skillet over medium heat. Add the eggplant and onion, and cook until softened, about 7 minutes. Add the capers and olives, season with salt and ¼ to ½ teaspoon peperoncino, and cook until the mixture is sizzling, about 1 minute. Add the tomatoes and 1 cup water. Sprinkle in the oregano. Simmer rapidly until slightly thickened and flavorful, about 15 minutes.

Break or slide the eggs into the skillet (see headnote), spacing them evenly. Cover and cook over medium heat until the eggs are cooked to your liking, 5 to 6 minutes for firm whites with slightly runny yolks. Sprinkle with the basil, grate the pecorino over the top, and serve.

Boiled Dandelion Greens, Tuna, and Egg Salad

Insalata di Cicoria, Tonno, e Uova Sode

SERVES 4 • You'll see hard-boiled eggs in lots of recipes in this book. I always have them on hand in my refrigerator for a quick snack or to add to sandwiches or salads, like this one. To hard-boil eggs perfectly, I start them in cold water to cover. Once the water comes to a simmer, I turn the heat to the lowest setting and simmer for 10 minutes, then remove the eggs directly to an ice bath. This recipe brings back memories of when, in springtime, I would go with my maternal grandmother, Rosa, to forage for wild dandelions. She would make soups and risottos and dress pasta with what we picked, but what I liked the most was this salad, which she made both with and without the canned tuna.

Active Time: 25 minutes
(includes cooking the eggs)

Total Time: 25 minutes

Kosher salt

1 pound dandelion greens, trimmed and cut into 1-inch pieces

¼ cup sliced almonds

4 tablespoons red wine vinegar

½ cup extra-virgin olive oil

Freshly ground black pepper

6 large eggs, hard-boiled (see headnote)

Two 5-ounce cans Italian tuna in oil, drained

Bring a large pot of salted water to a boil. Add the dandelion greens. Simmer until tender, 10 to 12 minutes. Transfer to an ice bath to cool. Drain, and pat very dry.

Put the almonds in a mini–food processor and pulse until crumbly. Add the vinegar, and pulse to make a chunky paste. With the machine running, add the olive oil in a slow, steady stream to make a very thick dressing. With the processor still running, add water a tablespoon at a time (up to 4 tablespoons) to make a dressing you can drizzle with a spoon. Season with ½ teaspoon salt and several grinds of black pepper.

Peel the eggs, and coarsely chop them. Add them and the tuna to a serving bowl with the greens. Drizzle with the dressing, season with salt and pepper, and toss well. Serve.

Vegetable Soup with Poached Eggs

Zuppa di Verdura con Uova in Camicia

SERVES 6 • You can also serve this soup ladled into ovenproof bowls with a slice of toasted bread in the bottom. Break an egg into each, and bake at 375 degrees until the eggs are set to your liking, 10 to 15 minutes. This works well if you have guests over; they all get their own bowls hot from the oven. Even without the eggs, this stands alone as a hearty vegetable soup.

Active Time: 30 minutes

Total Time: 1 hour 25 minutes

1 medium onion, cut into chunks

1 large carrot, cut into chunks

2 stalks celery, cut into chunks

1 cup loosely packed fresh Italian parsley leaves

4 garlic cloves, crushed and peeled

1 bunch white-stemmed Swiss chard, trimmed, tender stems and leaves separated, stems chopped, leaves coarsely chopped

½ cup extra-virgin olive oil, plus more for drizzling

2 tablespoons tomato paste

Kosher salt

Peperoncino flakes

2 fresh bay leaves

6 large eggs

6 slices country bread, toasted

½ cup freshly grated Grana Padano

Put the onion, carrot, celery, parsley, garlic, and chard stems in the work bowl of a food processor. Process to make a smooth paste or *pestata*. Heat the olive oil in a shallow Dutch oven over medium-high heat. Add the *pestata*, and cook, stirring, until the *pestata* dries out and sticks slightly to the bottom of the pot, about 10 minutes. Make a space in the pan, and add the tomato paste to that spot. Cook and stir the tomato paste there for a minute; then stir it into the *pestata*. Add 3 quarts cold water. Season with 2 teaspoons salt and a liberal amount of peperoncino. Add the bay leaves. Bring to a rapid simmer, and cook until reduced by about a third, about 40 minutes.

Add the chard leaves, and simmer until they're tender, about 15 minutes. Bring the soup to a light boil, and break in the eggs, leaving space between them. Cover, and simmer until the whites are set and the yolks are still runny, about 8 minutes.

To serve, remove the bay leaves, and put a slice of toasted bread in each bowl. Spoon in an egg, and ladle the soup over the bread and egg. Sprinkle with the cheese, and serve.

Breakfast Risotto

Risotto di Colazione

SERVES 4 TO 6 • Risotto for breakfast (or brunch)? Why not? I also like to make a simple risotto like this for dinner during the week, because these are all ingredients I (and likely you, too) have on hand in my pantry and refrigerator. Any leftovers make a good base for Risotto Cakes (page 97).

Active Time: 35 minutes

Total Time: 35 minutes

¼ cup extra-virgin olive oil

4 ounces slab bacon, cut into lardons

1 small onion, chopped

1 red bell pepper, chopped

1½ cups Arborio or other short-grain Italian rice

Kosher salt

Freshly ground black pepper

¾ cup dry white wine

6 to 7 cups hot chicken stock, preferably homemade, or water

2 large eggs

3 scallions, chopped, green parts included

½ cup freshly grated Grana Padano

Heat the olive oil in a large skillet over medium heat. Add the bacon, and cook until the fat is rendered and the bacon begins to crisp, about 3 minutes. Add the onion and bell pepper, and cook until tender, about 4 minutes. Add the rice, and stir to coat it in the oil. Cook until the rice grains are somewhat translucent, 1 to 2 minutes. Season with salt and pepper.

Add the white wine, and cook until it's absorbed. Ladle in enough hot stock to cover the rice. Simmer until the liquid is absorbed. Continue adding stock to cover as it is absorbed until the risotto is barely al dente, about 16 minutes from the first addition of liquid. Meanwhile, whisk the eggs in a small bowl with a pinch of salt. Whisk in 1 cup hot stock. Stir the eggs into the risotto to make wisps of scrambled eggs. Stir in the scallions and cook until they wilt, about 1 minute. Off heat, stir in the grated cheese. Serve immediately.

Cauliflower and Butternut Squash Hash

Pasticcio di Cavolfiori e Zucca

SERVES 4 TO 6 • This is another recipe that you can adapt to suit your tastes and what you have on hand. Instead of cauliflower, try another cruciferous vegetable—like Brussels sprouts or broccoli. Instead of butternut squash, use chunks of acorn, delicata, or kabocha squash. Any good melting cheese, like fontina, mozzarella, or cheddar, could stand in for the provolone. Crumbled sausage would be a welcome addition, too.

Active Time: 15 minutes

Total Time: 1 hour 10 minutes

½ medium head cauliflower, broken into large florets

1½ pounds butternut squash, peeled, seeded, and cut into 1-inch cubes

1 medium onion, cut into chunks

2 teaspoons chopped fresh thyme leaves

3 tablespoons extra-virgin olive oil

Kosher salt

Freshly ground black pepper

6 large eggs

1 cup freshly grated mild provolone

¼ cup freshly grated Grana Padano

2 tablespoons chopped fresh Italian parsley

Preheat the oven to 400 degrees. Scatter the cauliflower, butternut squash, and onion in a large oval gratin dish. Sprinkle with the thyme, and drizzle with the olive oil. Season with salt and pepper, and toss well. Pour ¼ cup water over the vegetables in the gratin dish. Bake until the cauliflower and squash are very tender, 35 to 40 minutes.

Remove the gratin dish from the oven. Lightly mash the vegetables with the back of a large spoon, leaving them rather chunky. Make six indentations into the mashed vegetables with the back of the spoon. Break an egg into each. Sprinkle with the provolone and Grana Padano. Return the dish to the oven, and bake until the eggs are cooked to your liking, 10 to 15 minutes for set whites with still-runny yolks. Sprinkle with the parsley, and serve.

Spinach and Fontina Casserole

Spinaci e Fontina in Casseruola

SERVES 6 TO 8 • You can assemble the casserole the night before you plan to serve it; just cover and refrigerate. Remove from the refrigerator about an hour before you're ready to bake, to let it return to room temperature. Coating the dish with butter and panko bread crumbs will assure a crispy edge to contrast with the moist interior.

Active Time: 10 minutes

Total Time: 1 hour 45 minutes
(includes thawing and resting time)

Unsalted butter, for the baking dish

Panko bread crumbs, for the baking dish

1-pound bag frozen spinach, thawed

8 large eggs

2 cups half-and-half

Kosher salt

Freshly ground black pepper

1 bunch scallions, chopped, green parts included

1 cup frozen peas, thawed

½ cup freshly grated Grana Padano

6 cups day-old crustless bread cubes

1 cup freshly grated Italian fontina

Preheat the oven to 350 degrees. Butter a 9-by-13-inch baking dish. Sprinkle with panko bread crumbs, and turn to coat the dish with the crumbs. Squeeze the spinach very dry in a kitchen towel (or press in a ricer), and chop. Beat the eggs and half-and-half in a large bowl until smooth. Season with 1 teaspoon salt and several grinds of pepper. Add the spinach, scallions, and peas to the bowl. Stir in ¼ cup of the Grana Padano and the bread cubes, and let soak for 10 minutes.

Pour the mixture into the prepared baking dish. Sprinkle with the fontina, and add the remaining Grana Padano. Bake until the casserole is set and the cheese is browned, 45 to 50 minutes. Let rest for 10 minutes before cutting into squares to serve.

SOUPS

Lentil and Pasta Soup 24
Pasta e Lenticchie

Stracciatella with Chicken and Vegetables 25
Stracciatella con Pollo e Verdure

Spicy Seafood Soup 26
Minestra Piccante di Pesce

Turkey, Mushroom, Chestnut, and Barley Soup 28
Zuppa di Tacchino con Funghi, Castagne, ed Orzo

Sauerkraut, Bean, and Pork Soup 29
Zuppa di Crauti, Fagioli, e Maiale

Salmon, Rice, and Leek Soup 31
Minestra di Salmone, Riso, e Porri

Summer Minestrone 32
Minestrone Estivo

Winter Minestrone 33
Minestrone Invernale

Onion Soup with Bread and Fontina Pasticciata 34
Zuppa di Cipolle, Pane, e Fontina Pasticciata

Wedding Soup 36
Zuppa Maritata

Cauliflower and Tomato Soup 37
Zuppa di Pomodoro con Cavolfiori

Tomato and Bread Soup with Scallops 38
Pappa al Pomodoro con Capesante

Shrimp, Swiss Chard, and Potato Chowder 39
Zuppa di Gamberi, Bietole, e Patate

When I make soup, I always make a big batch, so these recipes all make enough for several meals. Soups keep well in the refrigerator for a full week, but I like to freeze them in one-quart or one-pint plastic containers. Let the soup cool to room temperature before you put it in the containers, and always write the date and the kind of soup on the lid. This way you can rotate them and serve them for those last-minute, unplanned situations, or whenever you want a quick, easy meal.

When you first read one of my soup recipes, you may be startled at the amount of liquid it calls for in relation to other ingredients. For me, the best soups are ones that have had enough time to cook down and concentrate the flavors. Even if you begin with simple ingredients, when they have time to simmer together in the pot, you'll end up with a velvety soup full of flavor. Don't be afraid to cook these soups at a rapid simmer, as I do in my own kitchen. It breaks up the vegetables a bit more and helps the liquid evaporate. Just make sure to stir often, getting to the bottom and the corners of the pot, to make sure it's not sticking.

At home, I often serve soup as a whole meal, flanked by some garlic bread or grilled cheese toast. If you want to make these recipes more substantial, get creative and add a kielbasa to the Lentil and Pasta Soup (page 24), or a few sausages to the Summer (page 32) or Winter (page 33) Minestrone, and you have the equivalent of a hearty two-course meal. You can serve the soup as the first course and then the kielbasa or other sausage with some salad as the second course. Soup can fill the role of an appetizer as well. When you have guests coming over, pull it out of the freezer and heat it until piping hot, drizzle it with some extra-virgin olive oil and grated Grana Padano, and your first course is done.

Lentil and Pasta Soup

Pasta e Lenticchie

SERVES 8 TO 10 • If you're not going to serve all of this soup at one time, cook up until the step where you add the pasta. Add pasta only to what you're eating right away. Reserve and refrigerate or freeze what you'd like for leftovers, and add cooked pasta when you heat it up at a later time.

Active Time: 30 minutes

Total Time: 2 hours

3 tablespoons extra-virgin olive oil, plus more for drizzling

4 ounces pancetta, diced

1 onion, chopped

2 medium carrots, chopped

2 stalks celery, chopped

2 sprigs fresh rosemary

2 fresh bay leaves

One 28-ounce can whole San Marzano tomatoes, crushed by hand

1 piece Grana Padano rind (about 2 by 4 inches)

1 pound brown lentils, rinsed

Kosher salt

Peperoncino flakes

2 cups small pasta shapes, such as ditalini or orzo

Freshly grated Grana Padano or pecorino, for serving

Heat the olive oil in a large Dutch oven over medium heat. Add the pancetta, and cook until the fat begins to render, about 4 minutes. Add the onion, carrots, and celery, and cook until they've started to soften, about 4 minutes. Add the rosemary and bay leaves; then pour in the tomatoes, 4 quarts cold water, and the cheese rind. Bring it to a simmer, and simmer rapidly until the soup thickens and reduces by about a quarter, 50 minutes to 1 hour.

Add the lentils, and season with 2 teaspoons salt and a pinch of peperoncino. Simmer until the lentils are tender and the soup is thick and flavorful, 25 to 30 minutes more. Add the pasta, and cook until al dente— 7 to 8 minutes, depending on the shape. Remove the cheese rind, bay leaves, and rosemary sprigs. Serve with a drizzle of olive oil and some grated cheese.

Stracciatella with Chicken and Vegetables

Stracciatella con Pollo e Verdure

SERVES 6 TO 8 • To make this soup even heartier, add some rice in the last 15 minutes of cooking time. You can also stir in leftover cooked rice or other cooked grains you have on hand.

To defat soup stock, use a spoon to skim the top layer of fat from the cooled broth—or invest in a fat-straining measuring cup to make the job a lot easier.

Active Time: 25 minutes

Total Time: 2 hours

1 small chicken (about 2½ pounds)

3 stalks celery, cut into chunks

2 small onions, quartered

2 large carrots, cut into chunks

1 tablespoon tomato paste

Handful of fresh Italian parsley, leaves or stems

1 teaspoon black peppercorns

2 fresh bay leaves

Kosher salt

Freshly ground black pepper

2 large eggs

6 cups mature spinach leaves, chopped

Freshly grated Grana Padano or pecorino, for serving

Put the chicken in a pot large enough to hold it while leaving a few inches of space around the sides. Add the celery, onions, carrots, tomato paste, parsley, peppercorns, and bay leaves, and add water to cover by 2 inches, about 4 quarts. Bring to a simmer over medium-low heat. Set the lid ajar, and simmer rapidly until the chicken is very tender, about 1½ hours.

Strain the broth, and return it to the pot. When the chicken is cool enough to handle, shred the meat, discarding the skin and bones. Reserve the celery and carrots, and dice them.

Defat the broth, season with 2 teaspoons salt, and return to a rapid simmer. Cook until very flavorful and reduced to about 2 quarts. Season with salt and pepper. Beat the eggs in a spouted measuring cup with a pinch of salt and several grinds of pepper. Still whisking, drizzle a third of the egg mixture into the simmering soup. Add the remaining eggs in two more batches, letting the soup return to a simmer after each addition. Add the chicken meat, spinach, and diced vegetables. Return to a simmer to wilt the spinach and heat through, about 2 minutes. Remove the bay leaves. Serve, passing grated cheese at the table.

Spicy Seafood Soup

Minestra Piccante di Pesce

SERVES 6 • The addition of pasta makes this a stick-to-your-ribs kind of soup. For a somewhat lighter option, you can omit the pasta, leave the soup brothier, and serve it with grilled bread. The seafood listed here are suggestions, but you can use what looks freshest at your fish market. I'd stay away from oily fish, like salmon, or ones that break apart too easily, like flounder, but otherwise feel free to experiment. It is essential not to overcook the shellfish, so timing is important.

Active Time: 30 minutes

Total Time: 50 minutes

⅓ cup extra-virgin olive oil

12 ounces monkfish, cut into 1-inch cubes

Kosher salt

All-purpose flour, for dredging

1 medium onion, chopped

1 red bell pepper, chopped

Peperoncino flakes

1 cup dry white wine

One 28-ounce can whole San Marzano tomatoes, crushed by hand

3 sprigs fresh thyme

2 fresh bay leaves

8 ounces ditalini (or any other small pasta, like orzo or fregola)

1 pound manila clams

2 pounds mussels, scrubbed

8 ounces crabmeat, picked over for shells

2 tablespoons chopped fresh Italian parsley

Heat the olive oil in a large Dutch oven over medium-high heat. Season the monkfish with salt, and lightly dredge in flour. Add the monkfish to the oil, and brown all over, about 4 minutes. Remove to a plate.

Add the onion and bell pepper to the oil, over medium heat. Cook until slightly softened, about 4 minutes. Season with ¼ teaspoon peperoncino (or more, if you'd like your soup to be very spicy), and add the white wine. Simmer until it's reduced by half, about 2 minutes. Add the tomatoes and 4 cups water. Submerge the thyme and bay leaves in the sauce, and season with 1 teaspoon salt. Simmer until slightly thickened, about 20 minutes.

Add the pasta, and simmer for 2 minutes. Add the monkfish and clams, and simmer until the clams begin to open, about 3 minutes. Add the mussels, and simmer until the pasta is al dente and all of the shellfish have opened, discarding any that do not, 4 to 5 minutes more. Stir in the crabmeat, and simmer to heat through. Remove the bay leaves and thyme stems. Stir in the parsley, and serve.

Turkey, Mushroom, Chestnut, and Barley Soup

Zuppa di Tacchino con Funghi, Castagne, ed Orzo

SERVES 8 • The chestnuts in this soup are the secret ingredient that makes it so special. They break down as they cook, giving the soup a thick, almost creamy texture, without the addition of any cream at all. You can purchase cooked, peeled chestnuts in jars or cryovac packages at specialty food stores and some Italian markets, or even online. They will keep in your pantry for up to a year and are a wonderful addition, not just to soups but also to stews, stuffings, and braised meats.

Active Time: 35 minutes

Total Time: 2 hours 15 minutes

½ cup dried porcini

1 cup hot water

1 medium onion, chopped

2 stalks celery, chopped

1 medium carrot, chopped

⅓ cup extra-virgin olive oil, plus more for drizzling

2 bone-in, skin-on turkey thighs (about 2 pounds)

Kosher salt

1 pound assorted fresh wild mushrooms (cremini, shiitake, oyster, chanterelle, etc.), stems removed, thickly sliced

2 teaspoons chopped fresh thyme leaves

2 fresh bay leaves

8 ounces peeled, cooked chestnuts, coarsely chopped (about 1½ cups)

1 cup pearled barley, rinsed and drained

Freshly grated Grana Padano or pecorino, for serving

Put the dried porcini in a spouted measuring cup, and add 1 cup very hot water. Let them soak until softened, about 10 minutes. Drain, reserving the water, and chop and set aside the mushrooms.

Combine the onion, celery, and carrot in the work bowl of a food processor, and pulse to make an almost smooth *pestata*.

Heat the olive oil in a large Dutch oven over medium heat. Season the turkey with salt, and cook, skin side down, until browned, and then cook the other side, about 5 minutes on each side. Remove to a plate. Add the *pestata*, and cook until it begins to dry out and sticks to the bottom of the pot, 6 to 8 minutes. Add the fresh mushrooms, and cook, stirring occasionally, until the mushrooms are browned, about 8 minutes. Add the thyme, and stir. Add the bay leaves, 4 quarts water, and the porcini and their soaking liquid. Once the water is simmering rapidly, add the turkey and chestnuts, and cook until the turkey is tender, 1 to 1½ hours.

Remove the turkey, and let it cool. Add the barley, and cook until tender, 45 minutes to an hour. When the turkey is cool enough to handle, shred the meat, discarding the skin and bones. Add the shredded turkey back to the soup, and simmer to heat through. Remove the bay leaves. Serve with grated cheese and a drizzle of olive oil.

Sauerkraut, Bean, and Pork Soup

Zuppa di Crauti, Fagioli, e Maiale

SERVES 8 TO 10 • Depending on the brand, some sauerkrauts are more sour than others. For me, this soup is best with just a nice, sour edge to it—so drain and taste your sauerkraut before adding. If it is not very sour to begin with, it needs just a quick rinse. Kraut that is more sour should be rinsed twice, more thoroughly. This is a typical soup from Trieste, which my family and I ate all the time during the cold winter months when I was growing up.

Active Time: 20 minutes

Total Time: 3 hours (plus soaking time)

2 cups dried borlotti or cranberry beans, soaked overnight in water

1 large carrot, chopped

1 medium onion, chopped

4 garlic cloves, crushed and peeled

¼ cup extra-virgin olive oil, plus more for drizzling

Peperoncino flakes

3 fresh bay leaves

1½ pounds smoked pork butt or ham hocks, rinsed well with hot water

2 pounds sauerkraut, rinsed well (see headnote)

3 or 4 large russet potatoes, peeled (about 2 pounds)

Kosher salt

Drain the soaked beans. Put the carrot, onion, and garlic in the work bowl of a food processor, and pulse to make a *pestata*. Heat a large Dutch oven over medium heat. Add the olive oil. When the oil is hot, add the *pestata*, and cook until it starts to stick to the bottom of the pot, 6 to 8 minutes, stirring regularly. Season with peperoncino. Add the beans and bay leaves and 5 quarts water. Bring to a simmer, and add the smoked pork. Simmer rapidly until the beans are just tender, about 1 hour.

Add the sauerkraut and potatoes. Simmer rapidly, uncovered, until the beans and potatoes are very tender and the soup is flavorful, 1 to 1½ hours. Remove the potatoes and pork, keeping the soup warm. Put the potatoes in a bowl and mash coarsely. Add them back to the soup. Remove the meat from the pork bone and coarsely chop it. Add that back to the soup. Simmer to heat through. Remove the bay leaves. Season with salt, if needed. Serve with a drizzle of olive oil.

Salmon, Rice, and Leek Soup

Minestra di Salmone, Riso, e Porri

SERVES 4 TO 6 • No need to use an expensive center cut of salmon for this dish. The thinner tail pieces are often cheaper and work just as well here. Fresh peas are wonderful if you can find them; just add them at the same time as the rice, because they require a little more cooking time than frozen peas.

Active Time: 25 minutes

Total Time: 60 minutes

¼ cup extra-virgin olive oil

2 tablespoons unsalted butter

3 leeks, white and light-green parts, thickly sliced

2 stalks celery, chopped

Kosher salt

1 cup Arborio or other short-grain Italian rice

1½ cups frozen peas, thawed

1 pound skinless salmon fillets, cut into 1-inch chunks

4 scallions, chopped

Freshly ground black pepper, for serving

Heat the olive oil and butter over medium heat in a medium Dutch oven. When the butter is melted, add the leeks and celery. Season with 1 teaspoon salt. Cook until the leeks are softened but not browned, about 4 minutes. Add 3 quarts water, and bring to a rapid simmer. Simmer until the soup base is slightly reduced, about 30 minutes.

Add the rice, and return to a simmer, stirring occasionally. After 5 minutes, add the peas. Simmer until the rice is almost al dente, about 5 minutes more. Add the salmon, and cook until it is cooked through and the rice is al dente, 5 to 7 minutes more (about 17 minutes total). Stir in the scallions. Season with salt and pepper, and serve.

Summer Minestrone

Minestrone Estivo

SERVES 8 TO 10 • This soup is meant to showcase the vegetables of summer, so feel free to vary, based on what is good at your farmers' market—green beans, yellow squash, or even a handful of cherry tomatoes would be a wonderful addition here. If you're starting with favas in the pod, you'll need about 4 pounds or so to get the yield below. But don't worry—make it a family affair and you'll have them shucked and peeled in no time.

Active Time: 50 minutes

Total Time: 1 hour 50 minutes

½ cup extra-virgin olive oil

1½ pounds Yukon Gold potatoes, peeled and cubed

2 tablespoons tomato paste

2 leeks, white and light-green parts, halved lengthwise and thinly sliced

2 carrots, chopped

2 stalks celery, chopped

2 fresh bay leaves

3 ears corn, kernels removed from the cob, cobs reserved and broken in half

Kosher salt

Peperoncino flakes

2 medium zucchini, chopped

2 cups shelled fresh favas (see headnote; frozen peeled favas are okay, too)

4 cups loosely packed fresh basil leaves

¼ cup pine nuts, toasted

2 garlic cloves, crushed and peeled

Freshly grated Grana Padano or pecorino, for serving

Heat ¼ cup of the olive oil in a large Dutch oven over medium heat. Add the potatoes, and cook, stirring occasionally, until they're browned, 7 to 8 minutes. Make a spot in the center of the pot, and add the tomato paste in that spot. Cook and stir the tomato paste there until the tomato paste darkens a shade or two, about 1 minute. Add the leeks, carrots, and celery. Cook until the leeks wilt, 4 to 5 minutes. Add 4 quarts water, the bay leaves, and the corn cobs. Season with 2 teaspoons salt and a big pinch of peperoncino. Simmer rapidly until the vegetables are tender, about 30 minutes.

Add the zucchini and corn kernels. Adjust the heat so the soup is at a rapid simmer, and cook until zucchini and corn are tender, 15 to 20 minutes more. Add the favas, and simmer rapidly until they begin to break down and the soup is thick and flavorful, about 15 minutes more. Season with salt, and remove the bay leaves and the corn cobs.

Meanwhile, put the basil, pine nuts, garlic, and a pinch of salt in the work bowl of a mini–food processor and pulse to make a coarse paste. With the machine running, add the remaining ¼ cup olive oil, and process to make a smooth pesto. Stir the pesto into the soup just before serving. Pass grated cheese at the table.

Winter Minestrone

Minestrone Invernale

SERVES 8 TO 10 • As with my Summer Minestrone (preceding recipe), think of this recipe as a template for any hearty winter vegetable soup. You can vary the dried beans and include other vegetables—such as leeks, potatoes, sweet potatoes, turnips or rutabaga, parsnips, or myriad winter greens, like escarole, spinach, and chard.

Active Time: 40 minutes

Total Time: 2 hours 40 minutes
(plus soaking time)

4 ounces pancetta, chopped

4 garlic cloves, crushed and peeled

¼ cup extra-virgin olive oil, plus more for drizzling

1 medium onion, chopped

2 stalks celery, chopped

8 fresh sage leaves

1 tablespoon fresh thyme leaves

2 cups whole San Marzano tomatoes, crushed by hand

2 cups dried cannellini beans, soaked overnight, drained

1 pound green split peas, rinsed

2 fresh bay leaves

Kosher salt

Peperoncino flakes

2 large carrots, chopped

½ small head savoy cabbage, shredded

1 small butternut squash, peeled, seeded, and diced

1 bunch kale, finely chopped

Freshly grated Grana Padano or pecorino, for serving

Combine the pancetta and garlic in the work bowl of a food processor, and pulse to make a smooth *pestata*. Heat the olive oil in a large Dutch oven over medium heat. Add the *pestata*, and cook until the fat is rendered, about 4 minutes.

Meanwhile, combine the onion, celery, sage, and thyme in the same food processor (no need to wash it out), and pulse to make a second smooth *pestata*. Add this *pestata* to the pot, and cook until it dries out and begins to stick to the bottom of the pot, 6 to 7 minutes.

Add the tomatoes, beans, split peas, bay leaves, and 5 quarts water. Bring to a simmer, and adjust the heat so the soup is simmering rapidly. Cook, uncovered, until the split peas just begin to break down, about 30 minutes. Season with 1 tablespoon salt and a big pinch of peperoncino.

Add the carrots and cabbage, and simmer for 30 minutes more. Add the squash and kale. Simmer until all of the vegetables are tender and the soup is thick and flavorful, about 45 minutes to 1 hour more. Remove the bay leaves. Serve the soup with a drizzle of olive oil and a sprinkle of grated cheese.

Onion Soup with Bread and Fontina Pasticciata

Zuppa di Cipolle, Pane, e Fontina Pasticciata

SERVES 6 • Think of this as the Italian version of French onion soup. When we were testing this recipe in my kitchen, I had a box of mushrooms in my refrigerator and wanted to use them up. When we sat down to lunch that afternoon, and Tanya tasted the soup, she said, "I don't know why anyone hasn't thought of this before! Onion soup should always have mushrooms in it!"

Active Time: 45 minutes

Total Time: 1 hour 20 minutes

4 tablespoons unsalted butter

2 tablespoons extra-virgin olive oil

4 large sweet onions, thickly sliced

10 ounces white mushrooms, sliced

1 tablespoon chopped fresh thyme leaves

Kosher salt

Freshly ground black pepper

½ cup dry white wine

4 cups chicken stock, preferably homemade, or low-sodium store-bought

12 slices stale Italian bread, about ⅓ inch thick, from a long oval loaf

8 ounces Italian fontina, grated

¾ cup freshly grated Grana Padano

Preheat the oven to 425 degrees. Heat the butter and olive oil in a low, wide Dutch oven over medium-low heat. Add the onions, cover, and cook, stirring occasionally, until golden, 15 to 17 minutes. Add the mushrooms. Increase the heat to medium. Cook and stir until the mushrooms and onions are dark golden, about 10 minutes more. Add the thyme, and season with salt and pepper. Add the white wine, and simmer until it's almost completely reduced, about 2 minutes. Add the stock, and simmer until the onions are very tender and the soup is thick, 12 to 15 minutes.

Toast the bread on the oven rack until just golden, 3 to 4 minutes. Toss the fontina and Grana Padano together in a medium bowl. Set the pieces of bread on top of the soup, starting at the edges, then filling in the middle. Sprinkle with the cheese mixture. Bake in the oven until the cheese is browned and bubbly, about 20 minutes. Spoon the bread and soup into wide soup bowls to serve. This soup can also be poured into individual ramekins, then topped with the bread and cheese and baked.

Wedding Soup

Zuppa Maritata

SERVES 8 TO 10 • The little meatballs make this a hearty soup that is a meal in itself. To make it even heartier, you could add a handful of rice or a small pasta shape, like orzo or ditalini. A tip: preseasoned sausage meat also makes a quick and easy base for meatballs. This soup is also known as *zuppa di matrimonio*.

Active Time: 40 minutes
Total Time: 2 hours 15 minutes

Soup

1 onion, cut into chunks

2 stalks celery, cut into chunks

1 medium carrot, cut into chunks

4 garlic cloves, crushed and peeled

½ cup loosely packed fresh basil leaves

½ cup loosely packed fresh Italian parsley leaves

⅓ cup extra-virgin olive oil

2 fresh bay leaves

Kosher salt

Peperoncino flakes

1 large fennel bulb, trimmed, cored, and finely chopped

1 large bunch escarole, trimmed and cut into ½-inch shreds

1 large bunch spinach, stemmed and cut into ½-inch shreds

Meatballs

4 ounces day-old crustless country bread

1 pound sweet Italian sausage, removed from casings

2 large eggs, beaten

½ cup freshly grated mild provolone

½ cup freshly grated Grana Padano

¼ cup chopped fresh Italian parsley

Kosher salt

Freshly ground black pepper

Put the onion, celery, carrot, garlic, basil, and parsley in the work bowl of a food processor, and pulse to make a smooth *pestata*. Heat the olive oil in a large Dutch oven over medium-high heat. Add the *pestata*, and cook until it dries out and begins to stick to the bottom of the pot, 8 to 10 minutes. Add 5 quarts water and the bay leaves, and season with 2 teaspoons salt and a big pinch of peperoncino. Bring to a rapid simmer, and add the fennel. Simmer until the soup has reduced by about a quarter, 45 minutes to 1 hour.

Add the escarole and spinach, and continue to simmer until all of the vegetables are tender, and the soup has reduced by another inch or so, 20 to 30 minutes more.

Meanwhile, for the meatballs, put the bread in a large bowl and add water to cover. Soak until softened; then squeeze out the water. Return the squeezed-out bread to the bowl, and add the sausage, beaten eggs, provolone, Grana Padano, and parsley. Season lightly with salt and pepper. Mix well with your hands. Form into ¾-inch meatballs. Drop these into the soup toward the end, and poach until they're cooked through, about 15 minutes.

Remove the bay leaves from the soup, season with salt if needed, and serve.

Cauliflower and Tomato Soup

Zuppa di Pomodoro con Cavolfiori

SERVES 6 TO 8 • This vegetarian soup is substantial enough to please most meat eaters; however, you can also add some diced smoked sausage (like kielbasa) or shellfish (shrimp or scallops would be nice). Passata is a smooth tomato purée, available in grocery stores.

Active Time: 30 minutes

Total Time: 1 hour 40 minutes

1 large onion, coarsely chopped

3 stalks celery, coarsely chopped

2 garlic cloves, crushed and peeled

¼ cup extra-virgin olive oil

One 24-ounce jar tomato passata

2 fresh bay leaves

Kosher salt

Peperoncino flakes

2 large carrots, chopped

1 medium head cauliflower, broken into florets

1 cup Arborio or other short-grain Italian rice

2 cups frozen peas

Freshly grated Grana Padano or pecorino, for serving

Combine the onion, celery, and garlic in the work bowl of a food processor. Pulse to make a smooth *pestata*. Heat the olive oil in a medium Dutch oven over medium heat. Add the *pestata*. Cook and stir until the *pestata* dries out and begins to stick to the bottom of the pot, 6 to 7 minutes. Add the tomato passata and 3 quarts water. Add the bay leaves, and season with 2 teaspoons salt and a pinch of peperoncino. Bring to a rapid simmer. Add the carrots. Simmer until the liquid is reduced by about a quarter, about 30 minutes.

Add the cauliflower, and simmer until it begins to break down into the soup, about 45 minutes.

Add the rice, and simmer until it's almost al dente, about 10 minutes. Add the peas, and simmer until the rice is al dente, the peas are tender, and the soup is thick and flavorful, 5 to 7 minutes more. Remove the bay leaves. Serve with a sprinkle of Grana Padano.

Tomato and Bread Soup with Scallops

Pappa al Pomodoro con Capesante

SERVES 6 TO 8 • *Pappa al pomodoro* is a classic recipe in the Italian soup repertoire. In its most primal form, it can be made with just a few simple pantry ingredients. Here, I add scallops, for protein and to make this a whole meal in a bowl. You can substitute clams or mussels if you like, or a container of fresh crabmeat. You can also leave the seafood out entirely and still have a hearty, satisfying meal.

Active Time: 45 minutes

Total Time: 1 hour

⅓ cup extra-virgin olive oil

1 large onion, chopped

3 stalks celery, cut into ½-inch chunks

Kosher salt

Peperoncino flakes

1 cup dry white wine

Two 28-ounce cans whole San Marzano tomatoes, crushed by hand

3 leafy sprigs fresh basil

4 cups day-old crustless country-bread cubes

1 pound sea scallops, side muscle or "foot" removed, scallops halved vertically if large

Heat the olive oil in a medium Dutch oven over medium heat. Add the onion, and cook until it begins to wilt, about 3 minutes. Add the celery, and season with salt and a pinch of peperoncino. Pour in the white wine, and adjust the heat to bring the wine to a boil and cook until it's reduced by half, about 2 minutes.

Add the tomatoes, rinse the cans out with 4 cups water, and add to the soup. Submerge the basil sprigs in the soup, and bring to a simmer. Season with 1 teaspoon salt. Cover and simmer, mixing occasionally with a whisk until the tomatoes have broken down and the celery is tender, about 25 minutes.

Uncover the soup, and remove and discard the basil. Add the bread cubes, and return the soup to a simmer. Cook, using a sturdy whisk or wooden spoon to break up the bread cubes, until the soup is thick and flavorful, about 20 minutes. Stir in the scallops, simmer until they're just cooked through, 3 to 4 minutes, and serve.

Shrimp, Swiss Chard, and Potato Chowder

Zuppa di Gamberi, Bietole, e Patate

SERVES 6 TO 8 • In my kitchen, I am always looking for ways to enhance flavor and avoid waste. So, if you have the time, do as I do and use the trimmings from your celery, carrots, and leeks and the shrimp shells to make a quick stock with 3 quarts water. Just simmer them all together for 30 minutes or so, and strain. Of course, if you don't have time to do this, the chowder will be delicious nonetheless.

Active Time: 40 minutes

Total Time: 2 hours

¼ cup extra-virgin olive oil

2 pounds russet potatoes, peeled and cut into ½-inch chunks

4 garlic cloves, crushed and peeled

3 stalks celery, chopped

2 large carrots, chopped

2 leeks, white and light-green parts, halved and thinly sliced

1 large bunch white-stemmed Swiss chard, trimmed, leaves and tender stems separated, both chopped

Kosher salt

Peperoncino flakes

2 fresh bay leaves

1 pound large shrimp, peeled and deveined, tails removed, shrimp cut into chunks

Freshly grated Grana Padano or pecorino, for serving, if desired

Heat a large Dutch oven over medium-high heat. Add the olive oil. When the oil is hot, add the potatoes and garlic. Cook, stirring occasionally, until light golden and crusty, about 10 minutes. Reduce heat to medium. Add the celery, carrots, leeks, and chard stems, and cook until the leeks begin to wilt, about 5 minutes. Season with 1 teaspoon salt and a big pinch of peperoncino. Add 3 quarts water (or vegetable stock; see headnote). Add the bay leaves, and simmer rapidly until the broth has reduced by about a quarter and the flavors are concentrated, about 1 hour.

Add the chard leaves, and simmer until they're tender, 15 to 20 minutes more. Add the shrimp. Simmer until just cooked through, about 5 minutes. Remove the bay leaves, and season with salt to taste. Serve with a sprinkle of grated cheese, if desired.

SALADS

Tuna, Celery, and Warm Potato Salad 45
Insalata di Tonno, Sedano, e Patate Tiepide

Poached Chicken and Giardiniera Salad 46
Insalata di Pollo alla Giardiniera

Poached Seafood and Cannellini Bean Salad 48
Insalata di Mare con Cannellini

Smoked Chicken, Fennel, and Grapefruit Salad 49
Insalata di Pollo Affumicato con Finocchio e Pompelmo

Steamed Broccoli, Cannellini, and Egg Salad 51
Insalata di Broccoli, Cannellini, e Uova Sode

Striped Bass Salad with Zucchini and
Anchovy Dressing 52
Insalata di Spigola e Zucchine con Acciughe

Cod and Lentil Salad 54
Insalata di Baccalà e Lenticchie

"Antipasto" Rice Salad 55
Insalata di Riso

Roasted Squash and Carrot Salad with
Chickpeas and Almonds 57
*Insalata di Zucca Arrosto con Carote, Ceci,
e Mandorle*

Roasted Eggplant, Tomato, and Mozzarella
Salad with Salami 58
*Insalata di Melanzane e Pomodori al Forno
con Mozzarella e Salame*

Summer Panzanella 59
Panzanella Estiva

Winter Panzanella 60
Panzanella Invernale

Shaved Artichoke, Spinach, and Mortadella Salad 61
Insalata di Lamelle di Carciofi, Spinaci, e Mortadella

Salad of Radicchio, Endive, Apple, and Pecorino
with Cheese Toasts 62
*Insalata di Radicchio, Indivia, Mele, Pecorino, e Tostoni di
Formaggio*

Crab and Celery Root Salad 64
Insalata di Granchio e Sedano Rapa

Roast Beef, Potato, and Green Bean Salad 65
Insalata di Arrosto di Manzo con Patate e Fagiolini

Boiled Beef Salad 66
Bollito di Manzo in Insalata

Scallion, Asparagus, and Smoked Salmon 67
Salmone Affumicato con Asparagi e Scalogno

Shrimp and Melon Salad with Basil Mint Pesto 68
Insalata di Gamberi e Melone con Pesto di Menta

Dandelion and Chickpea Salad 69
Insalata di Cicoria e Ceci

For Italians, a salad is not just tossed greens. Seafood, meats, legumes, eggs, and certainly plenty of vegetables are frequently incorporated, often with the meats, fish, and vegetables cooked beforehand and tossed into the salad shortly before serving. In that tradition, in these recipes, I use a lot of cooked vegetables. The secret is to use one vessel to cook them, whether you are using just vegetables, or vegetables and seafood, or meat and vegetables. In most of these recipes, you need to be aware of the cooking time of each ingredient and sequence the cooking accordingly. Or cook one ingredient at a time, fish it out, and add the next. Compensate for the difference in cooking time by cutting the vegetables accordingly, bigger if they cook faster or smaller if they take longer to cook. Any way you cut them, salads make for tasty and nutritional meals.

As a child, I helped my grandma Rosa to tend her garden, and I especially liked to water her salad patch. She grew all kinds of different salad greens, but some of her favorites were butter lettuce and curly chicory, and she always had radicchio zuccherino, which is in the chicory family and has small green leaves. When Grandma's garden abounded with produce, in the summer, she would go to the farmers' market where she shared a stand with her neighbor Giovanna. They were neighbors in the small town of Busoler, in the outskirts of Pula, Istria.

The preparation for the market began the evening before; the sunset was late at that time of the year, and it was cool when we were getting the vegetables ready. Grandma would set barrels in the courtyard and fill them with cold water from the hose, one for each type of salad green. Then we would go to harvest the goodies. She would yank out the heads of lettuce first, the butter lettuce and the curly chicory, and would cut them at the root and set them in wooden boxes. One by one, we peeled off the damaged outer leaves and then threw the heads of lettuce into the barrel. This was the part I loved the most. I would take each lettuce head by the root part and gently dunk it in and out of the water until it was clean and all the earth had washed out of it, then put it in a wooden box lined with old newspapers, and nestle each one next to another. They looked like flowers! We covered them with damp burlap cloths. Grandma would also gather up other vegetables she had an excess of, such as zucchini, tomatoes, eggplant—whatever was in season—all washed and kept cool for the morning trip to the *mercato* in town, a 45-minute walk from home.

Every morning, the market was like a beehive—ladies meeting, greeting, buying, talking—but by around ten-thirty to eleven, it would all clear out. The ladies had to go home, lunch had to be ready: in a small city in those days, workingmen and -women would come home for lunch. This was when I got my reward: I was usually given some change to go buy an ice cream, or some watermelon, or a *Krapfen* (doughnut). Once I had my treat, I helped gather things together while Grandma would do some quick shopping herself. She had a deal with the owner of the trattoria on the corner, in which she would bring him the vegetables not sold and he would give her the old bread and table scraps, which she would bring home and feed to her pigs and chickens. Then we would gather our cart and slowly walk back to Busoler.

Tuna, Celery, and Warm Potato Salad

Insalata di Tonno, Sedano, e Patate Tiepide

SERVES 4 TO 6 • Boiled eggs always give an added dimension to a salad, and just 10 minutes of cooking will give you an egg with a hard-cooked yolk. If you prefer a yolk with a softer, jammier texture, simmer for 8 minutes. Tuna is a staple that is always in my pantry. I prefer the darker Italian tuna, canned in olive oil, over light tuna packed in water: it's moister and more flavorful.

Active Time: 40 minutes

Total Time: 40 minutes

2 pounds medium Yukon Gold potatoes

4 large eggs

Kosher salt

Freshly ground black pepper

1 small red onion, sliced

4 stalks celery, sliced, plus ½ cup celery leaves

Three 5-ounce cans Italian tuna in oil, drained

1 cup loosely packed fresh Italian parsley leaves, coarsely chopped

⅓ cup drained capers in brine

½ cup extra-virgin olive oil

¼ cup red wine vinegar

Bring the whole potatoes to a simmer in a large pot with the eggs. Simmer the eggs for 10 minutes, remove them to an ice bath, and continue cooking the potatoes until they're tender, 8 to 10 minutes more. Drain. Peel the eggs, and cut them into chunks.

Peel and cut the potatoes into chunks while they're still warm, and put them in a serving bowl. Season with salt and pepper. Add the red onion, celery and leaves, tuna, parsley, and capers. Drizzle with the oil and vinegar. Season again, and toss well. Add the chopped eggs, toss gently, and serve.

Poached Chicken and Giardiniera Salad

Insalata di Pollo alla Giardiniera

SERVES 4 • This great summer lunch dish will also give you some leftover stock to use for another meal. Reserve the cooking liquid from the chicken. After you've removed the meat, put the carcass back in the pot and simmer for another hour or so, and you've got a soup base that you can use in most of the soup recipes that call for chicken stock in the soup chapter, for an added flavor boost. I like this salad when the chicken is at room temperature, not cold from the refrigerator, but if you are making this dish for a buffet table, then chill the chicken before serving. What gives this dish its texture and freshness is the giardiniera. Giardiniera is a popular way of preserving and pickling hearty vegetables like carrots, celery, cauliflower, cipollini, and peppers for the winter and is served as an antipasto year round. It is easily made at home but you can find glass-jarred giardiniera at many markets and it is delicious.

Active Time: 25 minutes

Total Time: 2 hours (includes cooling time)

1 whole chicken (2½ to 3 pounds)

2 fresh bay leaves

Kosher salt

1 carrot, coarsely chopped

1 medium onion, coarsely chopped

1 stalk celery, coarsely chopped

½ cup fresh Italian parsley leaves, coarsely chopped, a handful of the stems reserved

2 cups giardiniera, drained and chopped

1 cup drained marinated artichoke heart quarters

1 pint grape tomatoes, halved

2 heads frisée, torn into bite-sized pieces

Freshly ground black pepper

⅓ cup extra-virgin olive oil

3 tablespoons red wine vinegar

Put the chicken in a large pot with water to cover by about 2 inches. Add the bay leaves, 2 teaspoons salt, the carrot, onion, celery, and parsley stems. Bring to a rapid simmer, and cook until the chicken is very tender, 1 hour to 1 hour 15 minutes. Let the chicken cool in the broth.

Remove the chicken, and discard the skin. Shred the meat into a large bowl.

Add the giardiniera, artichokes, tomatoes, parsley leaves, and frisée to the bowl with the chicken. Season with salt and pepper. Drizzle with the oil and vinegar, toss well, and serve.

Poached Seafood and Cannellini Bean Salad

Insalata di Mare con Cannellini

SERVES 6 TO 8 • I like canned beans, especially when you are in a pinch, but you can also make this salad with dried beans. Soak them overnight, drain, and add fresh water to cover, along with a few bay leaves and a generous drizzle of olive oil. Simmer until tender, usually about an hour, depending on the age of the beans. Season with salt only after the beans are cooked. Drain, remove the bay leaves, and let the beans cool for the salad.

Active Time: 30 minutes

Total Time: 40 minutes

Court Bouillon

½ cup dry white wine

Tough tops (outer leaves) from the fennel bulb used below

2 fresh bay leaves

1 teaspoon whole black peppercorns

Kosher salt

Salad

1 pound large shrimp, peeled and deveined

1 pound medium calamari, tubes and tentacles, tubes cut into ½-inch rings

2 pounds mussels, scrubbed

1 large fennel bulb, trimmed, halved, cored, and thinly sliced, plus ½ cup tender fronds

Two 15-ounce cans cannellini beans, rinsed and drained

½ medium red onion, thinly sliced

½ cup fresh Italian parsley leaves

Grated zest and juice of 1 lemon

⅓ cup extra-virgin olive oil

Kosher salt

Peperoncino flakes

For the court bouillon, combine 2 quarts water, the white wine, fennel tops, bay leaves, peppercorns, and 2 teaspoons salt in a medium Dutch oven. Bring to a simmer, and let simmer for 10 minutes to combine flavors. Remove and discard the fennel tops and bay leaves.

For the salad, add the shrimp to the court bouillon, and simmer until they curl and turn opaque, 2 to 3 minutes. Remove with a spider to a colander over a bowl to cool. Add the calamari to the court bouillon and simmer until just cooked, but still tender, 2 to 3 minutes. Fish it out and add it to the colander. Add the mussels to the court bouillon. Cover the pot, and cook until they open, discarding any that do not, 3 to 4 minutes. Remove them to the colander, and let cool. Reserve any cooking juices that have gathered in the bottom of the bowl.

Shuck the mussels from their shells, and put them in a large bowl with the shrimp and calamari. Add the sliced fennel, beans, red onion, and parsley. Sprinkle with the lemon zest and juice and olive oil, and season with salt and peperoncino. Toss well. If the salad seems dry, moisten with a few tablespoons of the reserved cooking juices and toss again. Chop the reserved fennel fronds, and sprinkle them over. Toss and serve.

Smoked Chicken, Fennel, and Grapefruit Salad

Insalata di Pollo Affumicato con Finocchio e Pompelmo

SERVES 4 • Don't forget about smoked meats when planning quick and easy weeknight dinners. Smoked chicken or turkey breast, pork loin, and smoked fish are all lean and flavorful and keep well in the refrigerator. Because they're so flavor-packed, a little goes a long way.

Active Time: 20 minutes

Total Time: 20 minutes

3 large pink grapefruits

1 medium fennel bulb, trimmed, halved, cored, and very thinly sliced, plus ½ cup tender fronds

½ red onion, thinly sliced

6 radishes, thinly sliced

2 tablespoons white wine vinegar

¼ cup extra-virgin olive oil

Kosher salt

Freshly ground black pepper

2 boneless, skinless smoked chicken breasts, julienned (about 1¼ pounds)

¼ cup sliced almonds, toasted

Cut the pith and peel from the grapefruits, and supreme the segments out of their membranes into a large bowl, catching all the juice. Squeeze the remaining juice from the grapefruit membranes into the bowl (you should get about ⅓ cup juice), and remove any seeds that might have fallen in. Add the fennel, red onion, and radishes. Drizzle with the vinegar and oil, season with salt and pepper, and toss well. Add the chicken, and toss again.

Sprinkle with the almonds and reserved fennel fronds. Serve.

Steamed Broccoli, Cannellini, and Egg Salad

Insalata di Broccoli, Cannellini, e Uova Sode

SERVES 4 • Never throw away your broccoli stems! You can peel and cook them along with the florets, as I do here, though they require a few extra minutes of cooking. You can also cut them into matchsticks and toss them with shredded carrots for a quick slaw, or cook them and purée them with potatoes for a new take on mashed potatoes. This dish is a great lunch or light dinner, or a new salad for your next buffet table. You can make it a bit more substantial by adding diced or julienned prosciutto cotto.

Active Time: 25 minutes
(includes cooking the eggs)

Total Time: 25 minutes

1 head broccoli, broken into florets, stem trimmed and peeled and cut into matchsticks

4 large eggs, hard-boiled

One 15-ounce can cannellini beans, rinsed and drained

½ red onion, sliced

¼ cup pitted oil-cured black olives, halved

⅓ cup extra-virgin olive oil

3 tablespoons red wine vinegar

Kosher salt

Freshly ground black pepper

Bring a large skillet of salted water to a boil. Add the broccoli stems, cover, and simmer for 3 minutes. Add the florets, and simmer until both are tender, about 5 minutes. Drain, and rinse under cold water in a colander.

Pat the broccoli dry. Peel the eggs, and set them aside. Put the broccoli in a serving bowl with the beans, onion, and olives. Drizzle with olive oil and vinegar. Season with salt and pepper. Toss well. Quarter the eggs, and add them to the bowl. Toss gently, and serve.

Striped Bass Salad with Zucchini and Anchovy Dressing

Insalata di Spigola e Zucchine con Acciughe

SERVES 4 • If you don't like anchovies, you can omit them from this dish, but they do add a savoriness that takes the mild flavors of bass and zucchini to a new level. When cooking fragile fillets, like the bass here, it's best to keep the skin on to prevent it from falling apart. Remove and discard the skin once you've cooked the fish. (Or give it to your cat!) Do not trim the ends from the zucchini before poaching, to keep it from absorbing water.

I compose this salad when the bass and zucchini are still warm, but it is also delicious, especially in the summer, when the bass and zucchini have been chilled in the fridge.

Active Time: 30 minutes

Total Time: 30 minutes

Kosher salt

2 fresh bay leaves

1 small onion, chopped

1 stalk celery, chopped

3 medium zucchini (about 1¼ pounds), left whole

4 skin-on striped bass fillets, halved crosswise

½ small red onion, thinly sliced

3 anchovy fillets, chopped

2 tablespoons white wine vinegar

¼ cup extra-virgin olive oil

Freshly ground black pepper

Bring 1½ quarts lightly salted water to a boil in a wide saucepan. Add the bay leaves, onion, and celery, and bring to a simmer. Add the zucchini, and return the water to a simmer. Simmer until the zucchini are just tender when pierced, 12 to 15 minutes. Remove the zucchini with a slotted spoon or spider, and dry.

Return the water to a simmer, add the bass, and simmer until just cooked through, about 5 minutes. Remove with a spider or slotted spoon, and dry. Season with salt.

Cut the zucchini into ½-inch half-moons, and put them in a large serving bowl. Add the red onion and anchovies. Remove the skin from the bass, and discard it. Break the fish into large pieces, and add them to the bowl. Drizzle with the vinegar and oil, and season with salt and pepper. Toss gently, and serve.

Cod and Lentil Salad

Insalata di Baccalà e Lenticchie

SERVES 6 • I love steaming fish. It's easy (especially in this recipe, since you've already got the pot of lentils simmering) and keeps the fish moist without adding fat. You could serve this salad on a bed of arugula or baby kale to add some crispness. I love it warm, but it is equally good at room temperature. This makes a satisfying meal or a main course anytime.

Active Time: 20 minutes
Total Time: 1 hour

2 fresh bay leaves

8 sprigs fresh thyme

1 large carrot, diced

1 stalk celery, diced

2 leeks, white and light-green parts, halved lengthwise and sliced ½ inch thick

1 pound brown lentils, rinsed

1 medium sweet potato, peeled and diced

Kosher salt

Freshly ground black pepper

1½ pounds skinless cod fillet, cut into 6 portions

1 cup loosely packed fresh Italian parsley leaves

¼ cup freshly squeezed lemon juice

¾ cup extra-virgin olive oil

Bring 2 quarts water to a boil in a medium Dutch oven. Add the bay leaves, half of the thyme, the carrot, and the celery. Simmer for 10 minutes to blend the flavors.

Add the leeks, lentils, and sweet potato. Simmer until the lentils are almost tender, about 30 minutes. Discard the thyme sprigs and bay leaves.

Season the broth with salt and pepper. Set a colander or strainer over the broth in the pot (it should fit in the pot with the lid on, without touching the liquid), and add the cod. Season the cod with salt and pepper, and lay the remaining thyme sprigs over it. Adjust the heat so the liquid is simmering, and cover the pot. Simmer until the cod is cooked through, about 10 minutes, remove it from the pot, and set it aside. Discard the thyme sprigs.

Meanwhile, combine the parsley and lemon juice in the work bowl of a mini–food processor. Season with salt and pepper. Process to a chunky paste. With the machine running, add the olive oil to make a smooth, slightly thick dressing.

Drain the lentils and other vegetables well. Put them in a large, shallow serving bowl. Drizzle with two-thirds of the parsley-and-lemon dressing, and toss well. Lay the cod on top. Drizzle with the remaining dressing, and serve warm.

"Antipasto" Rice Salad

Insalata di Riso

SERVES 6 TO 8 • Once the rice is cooked, draining and spreading it on a baking sheet will help it cool more quickly and prevent it from overcooking. Use this technique with any grain you're cooking for a salad. You could add leftover cooked chicken or seafood here as well. Or serve with slices of prosciutto on the side. This salad is ideal for a picnic or any other al fresco meal and can be served chilled or at room temperature. It's great for a buffet table as well.

Active Time: 15 minutes

Total Time: 50 minutes
(includes cooling time)

2 fresh bay leaves

Kosher salt

2 cups Arborio or other short-grain Italian rice

1 pound Campari tomatoes, cut into chunks

3 stalks celery, chopped

1½ cups drained marinated artichoke heart quarters, halved lengthwise

1 cup jarred roasted red peppers, cut into chunks

1 cup diced mild provolone (about 8 ounces)

1 cup pitted Gaeta olives, coarsely chopped

¼ cup drained capers in brine

¼ cup red wine vinegar

6 tablespoons extra-virgin olive oil

Peperoncino flakes

Bring 2 quarts water to a boil in a medium saucepan. Add the bay leaves and 1 teaspoon salt. Add the rice, and cook until it's al dente, 14 to 15 minutes. Drain the rice, and spread it on a baking sheet to cool, discarding the bay leaves.

When the rice is cool, put it in a large bowl. Add the tomatoes, celery, artichokes, peppers, provolone, olives, and capers. Drizzle with the vinegar and oil. Season with salt and a pinch of peperoncino. Toss well.

Roasted Squash and Carrot Salad with Chickpeas and Almonds

Insalata di Zucca Arrosto con Carote, Ceci, e Mandorle

SERVES 4 • I like to use tender, light-green escarole hearts in salads such as this one, but don't discard the darker and tougher outer leaves! They are perfect for braising, or shredded in soups. This is an ideal dish to make when we're transitioning from summer to fall, when the fall vegetables are in the market but the days are still warm enough to warrant a salad for dinner.

Active Time: 15 minutes

Total Time: 45 minutes

1 large acorn squash, or 2 small delicata squash, quartered, seeded, and sliced ½ inch thick

3 large carrots, cut into 1-inch chunks

1 teaspoon ground fennel seeds

5 tablespoons extra-virgin olive oil

Kosher salt

Freshly ground black pepper

One 15-ounce can chickpeas, rinsed and drained

2 tablespoons balsamic vinegar

2 escarole hearts, coarsely chopped

2-ounce piece ricotta salata

⅓ cup sliced almonds, toasted

Preheat the oven to 400 degrees with a baking sheet on the bottom rack. Toss the squash and carrots in a large bowl with the ground fennel and 2 tablespoons of the olive oil; season with ½ teaspoon salt and a generous grind of black pepper. Spread the vegetables on the baking sheet, and roast until almost tender, about 20 minutes. Set the bowl aside.

Add the chickpeas to the baking sheet with the squash and carrots, and drizzle with 1 tablespoon of the balsamic vinegar and 1 additional tablespoon of the olive oil. Stir to coat everything in the oil on the baking sheet, and continue to roast until the vegetables are browned and tender and the chickpeas have begun to crisp, 8 to 10 minutes more.

While they're still warm, put the contents of the baking sheet in the bowl used to toss the vegetables. Dress with the remaining tablespoon of the vinegar and remaining 2 tablespoons of the oil. Add the escarole, and toss well. Shred the ricotta salata over top with a vegetable peeler, and sprinkle with the toasted almonds. Serve immediately.

Roasted Eggplant, Tomato, and Mozzarella Salad with Salami

Insalata di Melanzane e Pomodori al Forno con Mozzarella e Salame

SERVES 4 • A meal in itself, this salad can also be an appetizer. For a hearty vegetarian meal, you can omit the salami (or serve it on the side for those who would like it).

Active Time: 15 minutes

Total Time: 45 minutes

2 medium Italian eggplants
(about 1¼ pounds total)

5 tablespoons extra-virgin olive oil

Kosher salt

3 cups grape or cherry tomatoes

½ teaspoon dried oregano, preferably Sicilian oregano on the branch

4 ounces smoked mozzarella or aged provolone, cubed

4 ounces thickly sliced salami, cut into matchsticks (optional)

¾ cup chopped jarred roasted red peppers

2 tablespoons drained capers in brine

2 tablespoons red wine vinegar

¼ cup loosely packed fresh basil leaves, roughly torn

Preheat the oven to 450 degrees. Peel the eggplant lengthwise with a vegetable peeler to make stripes. Cut the eggplant into 1-inch cubes, and spread them on a rimmed baking sheet. Drizzle with 3 tablespoons of the olive oil, season with ½ teaspoon salt, and toss. Roast until the eggplant is just golden, 15 to 20 minutes.

Add the tomatoes to the baking sheet, and toss with 1 more tablespoon of the oil. Roast until the eggplant is tender and the tomatoes are beginning to shrivel, about 10 minutes more.

Put the warm eggplant and tomatoes in a serving bowl, and sprinkle with the dried oregano. Toss well. Add the cheese, salami (if using), roasted peppers, and capers. Drizzle with the vinegar and the remaining tablespoon of the olive oil. Toss well. Add the torn basil leaves, toss, and serve warm.

Summer Panzanella

Panzanella Estiva

SERVES 4 • This salad is substantial enough as is for a summer meal, but feel free to add a couple of cans of drained Italian tuna in oil or shredded rotisserie chicken if you like. If you don't want to heat up your oven, you can also grill the vegetables. Just halve the zucchini lengthwise, then cube them after grilling. This salad is a great way to use up day-old bread. More than ever, we need to respect food and not waste it.

Active Time: 15 minutes

Total Time: 55 minutes

2 medium zucchini, cubed

2 small red onions, sliced into ½-inch-thick rings

8 tablespoons extra-virgin olive oil

Kosher salt

Freshly ground black pepper

1-pound piece day- or 2-day-old country bread, crust removed, cut into ½-inch cubes (about 6 cups)

1 pound ripe tomatoes, chopped (juices from chopping reserved)

2 Persian cucumbers, sliced

¼ cup red wine vinegar

2-ounce wedge Grana Padano, for shaving

Preheat the oven to 425 degrees with a baking sheet on the bottom rack. Toss the zucchini and onions in a large bowl with 2 tablespoons of the olive oil, and season with ½ teaspoon salt and several grinds of pepper. Spread the vegetables on the baking sheet, and roast, tossing halfway through, until nicely browned, 18 to 20 minutes. Let them cool on the baking sheet.

Put the cooled vegetables in the bowl you used to toss them in oil, and add the bread, tomatoes, and cucumbers. Drizzle with the vinegar and the remaining 6 tablespoons olive oil. (If the bread is dry, sprinkle with a little water first.) Let the salad stand for 10 to 20 minutes, so the bread can soak in the juices. Toss again, shave Grana Padano over the top, and serve.

Winter Panzanella

Panzanella Invernale

SERVES 4 TO 6 • If you want to add more protein to this salad, top each serving with a poached or fried egg.

Active Time: 15 minutes

Total Time: 1 hour 10 minutes

1 pound Brussels sprouts, trimmed and halved

1 delicata squash, quartered, seeded, cut into 1-inch chunks

½ small head cauliflower, broken into florets

7 tablespoons extra-virgin olive oil

2 teaspoons chopped fresh thyme leaves

Kosher salt

Freshly ground black pepper

8 ounces whole-grain bread, crust removed, cut into 1-inch cubes (about 4 cups)

½ cup chopped walnuts, toasted

3 to 4 tablespoons cider vinegar

6 cups loosely packed baby kale

Preheat the oven to 425 degrees with a baking sheet on the bottom rack. Toss the Brussels sprouts, squash, and cauliflower in a large bowl. Drizzle with 3 tablespoons of the olive oil, sprinkle with the thyme, ½ teaspoon salt, and several grinds of pepper. Spread the vegetables on the baking sheet, and roast until they're tender, 35 to 40 minutes, tossing halfway through. Let them cool slightly, about 5 minutes.

Put the warm vegetables in the bowl you used to toss them in oil, and add the bread and walnuts. Drizzle with 3 tablespoons of the vinegar and the remaining olive oil. (If the bread is dry, sprinkle with the remaining tablespoon vinegar and a little water.) Let the bread soak up the juices, about 10 minutes. Add the kale, and season with more salt and pepper if needed. Toss and serve.

Shaved Artichoke, Spinach, and Mortadella Salad

Insalata di Lamelle di Carciofi, Spinaci, e Mortadella

SERVES 4 • This is the salad to make when you find young, tender, chokeless baby artichokes. Don't attempt it if the artichokes are tough or past their prime. If needed, substitute Jerusalem artichokes, washed well and thinly sliced. If you don't have a mandoline, use a very sharp knife and thinly slice the artichokes by hand.

Active Time: 20 minutes

Total Time: 20 minutes

1 lemon

12 ounces baby artichokes (about 6)

3 stalks celery, very thinly sliced, plus ½ cup inner leaves

3-ounce chunk Grana Padano, grated on the coarse holes of a box grater

6-ounce chunk mortadella, cut into matchsticks

6 cups loosely packed baby spinach

¼ cup extra-virgin olive oil

Kosher salt

Freshly ground black pepper

Juice the lemon into a large serving bowl, and set aside.

Trim the stems, tough outer leaves, and tops from the artichokes. Halve them, and thinly slice on a mandoline into the large bowl with the lemon juice, tossing as you go. Add the celery, cheese, mortadella, and spinach. Drizzle with the olive oil, and season with salt and pepper. Toss well, and serve right away.

Salad of Radicchio, Endive, Apple, and Pecorino with Cheese Toasts

Insalata di Radicchio, Indivia, Mele, Pecorino, e Tostoni di Formaggio

SERVES 4 • These cheese toasts are a great accompaniment to most salads and soups. Think of them as an Italian grilled cheese, lighter and crispier than the diner version, but equally satisfying. You can vary the cheese, based on what you have; just use equal parts hard grating cheese (such as Grana Padano or pecorino) and a softer cheese (like cheddar or Italian fontina).

Active Time: 30 minutes

Total Time: 30 minutes

Toasts

¼ cup finely grated Italian fontina

¼ cup finely grated pecorino

Extra-virgin olive oil, for brushing the skillet

4 long, thin slices country bread (about 4 by 6 inches each)

Kosher salt

Freshly ground black pepper

Salad

2 tablespoons white wine vinegar

¼ cup extra-virgin olive oil

Kosher salt

Freshly ground black pepper

2 small heads radicchio, torn into bite-sized pieces

3 heads Belgian endive, sliced crosswise into ½-inch pieces

2 Granny Smith apples, cut into matchsticks

½ cup walnuts, coarsely chopped, toasted

2 ounces pecorino, cut into matchsticks

½ cup loosely packed fresh Italian parsley leaves

¼ cup coarsely chopped fresh chives

For the toasts, heat a large cast-iron skillet or griddle over medium-low heat. Combine the fontina and pecorino in a small bowl. Brush the preheated skillet lightly with olive oil. Add the bread slices in one layer, and let them sit until toasted and golden on the underside, 2 to 3 minutes. Flip, and toast the other side, 2 to 3 minutes. Season with salt and pepper, and sprinkle the tops with the cheese. Let it melt for a minute; then flip. Press with a spatula to weigh the bread down and compress it slightly. Cook until the cheese is crisp and toasted and no longer sticks to the bottom of the pan, 1 to 2 minutes.

For the salad, whisk the vinegar and oil together in a serving bowl. Season with salt and pepper. Add the radicchio, endives, apples, and walnuts, and toss well. Shave in the pecorino in long shards, using a vegetable peeler. Add the parsley and chives, and toss gently. Serve with the cheese toasts.

Crab and Celery Root Salad

Insalata di Granchio e Sedano Rapa

SERVES 4 • Though salting the vegetables is an extra step, it's worth the time. The salt extracts excess moisture from the celery root and carrots, keeping them crisp but concentrating their flavor. Crab is lovely here, but you could also use cooked shrimp or flakes of poached white fish, such as cod.

Active Time: 15 minutes

Total Time: 15 minutes

1 large celery root, peeled and julienned (on a mandoline, if you have one) (about 1 pound)

2 large carrots, julienned (on a mandoline, if you have one)

¼ cup white wine vinegar

Kosher salt

½ cup chopped fresh chives

3 tablespoons extra-virgin olive oil

1 tablespoon Dijon mustard

Freshly ground black pepper

1 pound lump crabmeat, picked over for shells

Combine the celery root and carrots in a large bowl. Drizzle with the vinegar, and sprinkle with 1 teaspoon salt. Toss well. Let sit for 30 minutes to soften the vegetables.

After 30 minutes, drain off and discard any excess liquid. Add the chives, olive oil, and mustard, and toss well to coat the vegetables. Season with salt and pepper, add the crabmeat, toss, and serve.

Roast Beef, Potato, and Green Bean Salad

Insalata di Arrosto di Manzo con Patate e Fagiolini

SERVES 4 TO 6 • Good-quality deli meats can be a lifesaver for weeknight meals. Roast beef, salami, prosciutto—you name it—they're all quick, delicious means to satisfy the meat eaters in your home, and including them in salads provides a hearty, healthy portion of vegetables. This salad is also a good way to use up leftover roast beef you might have in the fridge; just make sure you slice it thin.

Active Time: 15 minutes

Total Time: 55 minutes

1½ pounds Yukon Gold potatoes, cut into 1-inch chunks

12 ounces green beans, trimmed

5 tablespoons extra-virgin olive oil

2 teaspoons chopped fresh thyme leaves

Kosher salt

Freshly ground black pepper

3 scallions, including green parts, thinly sliced

¼ cup heavy cream

2 tablespoons drained prepared horseradish

2 tablespoons freshly squeezed lemon juice

1 tablespoon grainy mustard

1 pound thinly sliced rare deli roast beef or leftover rare roast beef

Preheat the oven to 425 degrees. Toss the potatoes and green beans on a rimmed baking sheet with 3 tablespoons of the olive oil, the thyme, 1 teaspoon kosher salt, and a generous grind of pepper. Pour ½ cup water onto the baking sheet, and roast on the bottom rack of the oven, stirring once or twice, until the water has evaporated and the vegetables are tender and golden, 30 to 40 minutes. Once the vegetables are out of the oven, sprinkle with the scallions, and toss.

Meanwhile, whisk the cream, horseradish, lemon juice, and mustard in a small bowl. Whisk in the remaining 2 tablespoons olive oil. Season with salt and pepper.

Mound the vegetable mixture in the middle of a serving platter. Drape the meat around the perimeter of the vegetables on the platter. Drizzle the meat and vegetables with about half of the dressing. Serve, with the remaining dressing on the side.

Boiled Beef Salad

Bollito di Manzo in Insalata

SERVES 6 • I am a big fan of the flat-iron roast. It comes from the shoulder of the cow and is nicely marbled with an intense beefiness; plus, it stays moist when cooking. Don't discard the liquid used to cook the beef. You can save it to use as a soup base, or to replace water when cooking grains.

In the recipe I list bottled horseradish, which is very good, but today most stores carry fresh horseradish root as well. If you can find it, buy it. It is a long root that you peel like a carrot with a potato peeler, then grate on a microplane just before using. It is intense, it will make you cry, and it is delicious and healthy. Whatever you do not use, wrap in plastic wrap and keep in the refrigerator.

Active Time: 20 minutes

Total Time: 3 hours 20 minutes (includes cooling time)

3-pound piece boneless beef flat-iron roast

3 large carrots, peeled and halved crosswise

2 stalks celery, halved crosswise

1 medium onion, halved

½ small bunch Italian parsley, leaves separated and chopped, stems reserved

2 fresh bay leaves

1 tablespoon tomato paste

1 teaspoon whole black peppercorns

Kosher salt

2 tablespoons red wine vinegar

1 tablespoon drained prepared horseradish

¼ cup extra-virgin olive oil

Freshly ground black pepper

½ cup cornichons, cut into chunks

½ small red onion, thinly sliced

4 radishes, thinly sliced

Put the beef, carrots, celery, onion, parsley stems, bay leaves, tomato paste, and peppercorns in a large Dutch oven with water to cover by about 2 inches. Season with 2 teaspoons salt. Simmer until the beef is very tender, about 2 hours. Let it cool in the broth. Strain. Remove the beef, carrots, and celery, and let them cool to room temperature.

Whisk the vinegar and horseradish in a serving bowl. Whisk in the olive oil to make a smooth dressing. Season with salt and pepper. Dice the beef, slice the carrots and celery, and add them to the bowl with the dressing. Add the chopped parsley leaves, cornichons, red onion, and radishes. Toss well, and serve.

Scallion, Asparagus, and Smoked Salmon

Salmone Affumicato con Asparagi e Scalogno

SERVES 4 TO 6 • You can cook the vegetables ahead of time, but don't dress them until the last minute: the vinegar will begin to discolor them and turn them drab after 5 minutes or so. I love smoked salmon. This would be a lovely brunch dish, but don't relegate smoked salmon to just the morning hours—it's a tasty and convenient addition to salads, sandwiches, and pizzas, too.

Active Time: 30 minutes

Total Time: 30 minutes
(includes cooking the eggs)

2 bunches asparagus (about 2 pounds)

1 bunch scallions, including green parts, trimmed

3 tablespoons white wine vinegar

⅓ cup extra-virgin olive oil

Kosher salt

Freshly ground black pepper

4 ounces baby watercress

4 eggs, hard-boiled, quartered

8 ounces sliced smoked salmon

Bring a large skillet of salted water to a boil. Break off the tough ends of the asparagus, and peel about a third of the way down on the base.

Add the asparagus and scallions to the skillet, and simmer until just tender, 5 to 6 minutes. Drain in a large colander, and run under cold water to stop the cooking. Toss a few cups of ice cubes on top to quicken the cooling process. Drain, and pat very dry.

Cut the asparagus and scallions into 2-inch pieces, and put them in a serving bowl. Drizzle with the vinegar and olive oil. Season with ½ teaspoon salt and several grinds of pepper, and toss well. Add the watercress, and toss again. Serve with the eggs and smoked salmon around the sides of the platter.

Shrimp and Melon Salad with Basil Mint Pesto

Insalata di Gamberi e Melone con Pesto di Menta

SERVES 4 • This dish is lovely with ripe summer melon, but feel free to try with other fruit as well—wedges of stone fruit such as peaches, nectarines, or plums would also be delicious.

Active Time: 25 minutes

Total Time: 25 minutes

Pesto

1 cup loosely packed fresh basil leaves

½ cup loosely packed fresh mint leaves

Kosher salt

1 tablespoon freshly squeezed lemon juice

⅓ cup extra-virgin olive oil

Salad

2 fresh bay leaves

Kosher salt

1 pound extra-large shrimp, peeled and deveined

½ small cantaloupe, peeled and cubed

½ small honeydew, peeled and cubed

2 stalks celery, thinly sliced on the bias, plus ½ cup tender leaves

2 little-gem lettuces, torn into bite-sized pieces

For the pesto, combine the basil and mint in the work bowl of a mini–food processor. Season with ½ teaspoon salt. Add the lemon juice, and pulse to make a chunky paste. With the machine running, add the oil to make a smooth pesto.

For the salad, put the bay leaves in a large Dutch oven with 2 quarts lightly salted water. Bring to a simmer. Add the shrimp, and simmer until they're just cooked through, 3 to 4 minutes. Drain, discarding the bay leaves, and cool the shrimp under running water. Pat them very dry.

Place the shrimp in a shallow serving bowl with the cantaloupe, honeydew, celery and celery leaves, and lettuce. Drizzle with about half of the pesto. Toss, drizzle the remaining pesto over the top, and serve.

Dandelion and Chickpea Salad

Insalata di Cicoria e Ceci

SERVES 4 • This simple, nourishing salad makes a great base for a variety of easy proteins—canned tuna, smoked fish, or poached chicken. If you haven't tried dandelion greens, this salad is a good place to start. To trim them, just remove and discard the tough bottoms of the stems and remove any browned spots on the leaves. Wash well—they can be very gritty. Their bright but somewhat bitter flavor is a great foil for starchy beans, like the chickpeas here. Sometimes in the spring, in vegetable markets, you might find wild dandelions; make sure you try them. They are sold by the pound as a small plant attached to the roots. Cut the roots off, and proceed to use the stems.

Active Time: 35 minutes

Total Time: 35 minutes
(includes cooking the eggs)

Kosher salt

2 bunches dandelion greens, trimmed
(about 2 pounds)

Two 15-ounce cans chickpeas, rinsed
and drained

2 tablespoons red wine vinegar

¼ cup extra-virgin olive oil

Freshly ground black pepper

Kosher salt

4 eggs, hard-boiled, very coarsely
chopped

Bring a large pot of salted water to a boil. Add the greens, and simmer until they're very tender, about 15 minutes. Drain them in a colander, and cool under running water. Pat dry, and coarsely chop.

Put the greens in a serving bowl, and add the chickpeas. Drizzle with the vinegar and oil. Season with salt and pepper, and toss well. Add the eggs, toss gently, and serve.

PASTAS, RISOTTOS, AND PIZZAS

Gnudi 75
Gnudi

Cavatappi with Asparagus and Spinach Pesto 78
Cavatappi con Pesto d'Asparagi e Spinaci

Gemelli with Classic Pesto, Potatoes, and Green Beans 79
Gemelli al Pesto

Spaghetti with Yellow Tomato Pesto 80
Spaghetti al Pesto di Pomodoro Giallo

Penne with Cauliflower and Green Olive Pesto 81
Penne con Cavolfiori e Pesto d'Olive Verdi

Mezzi Rigatoni with Raw Tomato Sauce 83
Mezzi Rigatoni al Pesto di Pomodoro Crudo

Fusilli with Salami and Roasted Peppers 84
Fusilli con Salame e Peperoni

Capellini with Spicy Tomato Crab Sauce 85
Capellini con Sugo di Granchio Piccante

Skillet Lasagna 86
Lasagna in Padella

No-Boil Stuffed Shells 88
Conchiglie Ripiene al Forno

Summer Tomato and Basil Risotto with Mozzarella 89
Risotto con Pomodoro, Mozzarella, e Basilico

Mushroom and Sausage Risotto 90
Risotto con Funghi e Salsicce

Seafood and Leek Risotto 91
Risotto di Mare con Porri

Zucchini, Peas, and Pancetta Risotto 93
Risotto con Zucchine, Piselli, e Pancetta

Oat Risotto 94
Risotto d'Avena ai Funghi Porcini

Barley and Chicken Risotto 95
Risotto di Farro con Pollo

Chicken and Rice 96
Riso con Pollo

Risotto Cakes 97
Riso al Salto

Pan Pizza 98
Pizza in Padella

Tomato and Zucchini Bread Lasagna 100
Lasagna di Pane con Pomodori e Zucchine

Pasta and risotto are the cornerstones of Italian family cooking and are ideally suited for one-pot cooking.

I grew up making and eating fresh pasta. In the north of Italy, fresh pasta is king; in the south, they prefer dried pasta. Although I love making and eating fresh pasta, today I prefer dried. I like the texture and the nutty flavor, and all the different shapes we have to choose from make it fun. Fresh pasta is usually made from soft wheat and eggs, whereas dried pasta is made from semolina flour, durum wheat, and water. There are about 350 different shapes of dried pasta, and some of these shapes have different names regionally.

Choosing the right shape of pasta to go with your sauce is important. A long, flat pasta such as spaghetti is great with thick tomato sauces and meat sauces; a tubular pasta will collect sauces in its nooks and crannies, and ridges on the pasta create a great mouthfeel. Short shapes are usually more appropriate for chunky sauces. When you buy dried pasta, look for these qualities: It should be made of 100 percent semolina flour, and the higher the protein the better; 17 percent is good. The pasta should not be shiny or blotchy, and it should not be cracked or broken. It should be opaque and rough to the touch. Imported Italian pasta is most likely to have the right characteristics. To cook dried pasta, always salt the water, and throw the pasta into the boiling water, give it a stir, and let it come back to boiling. Do not add oil to the pasta-cooking water, and do not rinse your pasta when it's cooked. I always undercook my pasta, and after draining it, I add it to the sauce to finish cooking; absorbing some of the sauce and its flavors makes the pasta taste better. If there is too much sauce, remove some and set it aside. If needed, I add some of the pasta-cooking water and stir the pasta until it is coated with the sauce and cooked to the right texture. Never oversauce your pasta: you can always add more sauce once you have plated it. Add freshly grated cheese when you are ready to serve. Remove the pasta from the heat before tossing in cheese, and bring extra grated cheese to the table.

As much as I love pasta, when it comes to one-pot meals, nothing beats risotto. One pot is all you need, but it needs to be a pot with certain characteristics. I like a wide skillet or braising pot—wide because the liquid added periodically to the rice needs to have the space to cook the rice evenly and evaporate regularly. The steady addition of liquid makes the risotto creamier. I prefer cast iron, or thick steel lined with ceramic, because a ceramic lining is a good buffer to keep the rice from scorching. The pot should not be deep. All the rice should be cooking at the same temperature, so it is all at the same texture, al dente, when done. Once you have found the right pot for you, it will be the one you will always use, your go-to tool for risotto. Do not forget to use a good sturdy wooden spoon with it.

Gnudi

Gnudi

SERVES 4 TO 6 • The ricotta should be quite dry to start here. I wouldn't use a commercial grocery-store brand. Seek out fresh whole-milk ricotta from a smaller purveyor or an Italian market. (You can also try making your own. It's easy, I promise!) If the ricotta you buy is still a little wet, drain it overnight in the refrigerator in a cheesecloth-lined strainer. If it is very dry, then you can skip this step.

Here I give you a sage-butter sauce to dress the gnudi, an easy and delicious sauce that you can use with many different pasta dishes. I also often dress gnudi with butter and a small amount of tomato sauce; if you do this, make sure you don't overdo the tomato sauce.

Active Time: 30 minutes

Total Time: 30 minutes

Gnudi

Kosher salt

2 pounds fresh ricotta, drained overnight if needed (see headnote)

2 large eggs, beaten

Grated zest of ½ lemon

Pinch of freshly grated nutmeg

1 cup freshly grated Grana Padano

½ cup chopped fresh Italian parsley

Freshly ground black pepper

¾ cup fine dry bread crumbs, plus more if needed

½ cup all-purpose flour, plus more for rolling

Sauce

1 stick unsalted butter

12 fresh sage leaves

Kosher salt

Bring a large pot of salted water to a boil to cook the gnudi. Choose a heatproof serving bowl that will fit inside the pot. Set the bowl aside for now.

For the gnudi, combine the ricotta, eggs, lemon zest, and nutmeg in a large bowl. Mix well to combine. Stir in the grated cheese and parsley. Season with 1 teaspoon salt and several grinds of pepper. Stir until smooth. Add the bread crumbs and flour. Mix until the mixture is blended and pulls off the sides of the bowl, and holds its shape if rolled into a ball. If the dough doesn't hold its shape, add a tablespoon more of bread crumbs, and mix again until it does. (Try not to overmix, though.)

Spread some more flour in a wide, shallow dish. With floured hands, scoop about 2 tablespoons of the mixture and roll into a ball. I would suggest you test one or two of the first gnudi you make, plopping them into the boiling water and letting them float to the top. If they remain whole, you are good to go; if not, you need some more flour in the dough. Continue with the remaining mixture—you should get about twenty-four balls—and set them on a sheet pan lined with a clean, floured kitchen towel. →

Freshly ground black pepper

½ cup freshly grated Grana Padano, for serving

For the sauce, combine the butter and sage in the serving bowl, and set over the boiling water until the butter melts. Set the bowl aside.

With the water boiling at a low roll, gently add the gnudi directly into the water. Stir gently and occasionally with a wooden spoon. Simmer until they float to the surface and are cooked through, 5 to 7 minutes.

Remove the gnudi with a spider to the bowl with the melted butter. Season with salt and pepper. Sprinkle with the grated cheese. Toss and serve.

Cavatappi with Asparagus and Spinach Pesto

Cavatappi con Pesto d'Asparagi e Spinaci

SERVES 6 • Pesto doesn't have to be made only with herbs—greens, such as baby kale or arugula, also work great. I like to combine them with one or two fresh herbs for a bright and balanced flavor. I also like to use different nuts in my pesto, sometimes pine nuts, sometimes almonds, sometimes walnuts; here I use pistachios.

Active Time: 25 minutes
Total Time: 25 minutes

Kosher salt

4 cups loosely packed baby spinach leaves

1 cup loosely packed fresh Italian parsley leaves

⅓ cup shelled unsalted pistachios, toasted

1 garlic clove, crushed and peeled

½ cup extra-virgin olive oil

Freshly ground black pepper

1 pound cavatappi

1 bunch medium-thickness asparagus, tough stems trimmed, bottoms peeled, stalks cut into 1-inch pieces

½ cup freshly grated pecorino

Bring a large pot of salted water to a boil for the pasta. Put the spinach, parsley, pistachios, and garlic in the work bowl of a food processor. Process to make a chunky paste. Add the olive oil with the machine running to make a smooth pesto. Transfer to a serving bowl. Season with ½ teaspoon salt and several grinds of black pepper.

Add the cavatappi to the boiling water and cook until al dente; add the asparagus in the last 4 minutes. Remove pasta and asparagus with a spider to the serving bowl. Sprinkle with the grated cheese. Toss to coat the pasta with the sauce, adding up to ½ cup pasta-cooking water if it seems dry, and serve.

Gemelli with Classic Pesto, Potatoes, and Green Beans

Gemelli al Pesto

SERVES 6 • When summer basil is plentiful, you can make a double or triple batch of pesto, because it freezes well. Make the pesto up until the addition of cheese. Pack in small zip-top freezer bags, squeeze out excess air, and freeze for up to 2 to 3 months. These bags of pesto will thaw in the refrigerator in a few hours and bring a taste of summer to the cooler months.

Active Time: 30 minutes

Total Time: 30 minutes

Kosher salt

2 cups loosely packed fresh basil leaves

1 cup loosely packed fresh Italian parsley leaves

¼ cup pine nuts, toasted

2 garlic cloves, crushed and peeled

½ cup extra-virgin olive oil

Freshly ground black pepper

12 ounces new potatoes, cut into ¾-inch chunks

1 pound gemelli

12 ounces green beans, trimmed and halved crosswise

½ cup freshly grated Grana Padano

Bring a large pot of salted water to a boil for the pasta. Put the basil, parsley, pine nuts, and garlic in a blender. Pulse to make a smooth paste, adding the olive oil in a steady stream as processing. Transfer to a bowl, and season with ½ teaspoon salt and several grinds of pepper.

Add the potatoes to the boiling water, and boil them for 5 minutes before adding the pasta. Cook the pasta until it's about halfway cooked, about 5 minutes. Add the green beans. Cook until the pasta is al dente and the vegetables are tender, about 7 minutes. Remove potatoes, pasta, and green beans with a spider to a large serving bowl. Add the pesto and grated cheese to the bowl. Season with salt and pepper; toss all well, adding up to ½ cup pasta-cooking water if it seems dry, and serve.

Spaghetti with Yellow Tomato Pesto

Spaghetti al Pesto di Pomodoro Giallo

SERVES 6 • In the summer, I grow many varieties of sweet cherry tomatoes, so they ripen at slightly different times, ensuring daily tomatoes for many weeks. Yellow tomatoes have slightly less acidity than red ones, which makes this uncooked sauce extra sweet. You can absolutely substitute red if you don't have yellow, though. As an added bonus, I toss finely diced zucchini into this sauce, and the heat of the pasta cooks it just enough to soften it without making it mushy.

Active Time: 25 minutes
Total Time: 25 minutes

Kosher salt

1 pint ripe yellow cherry tomatoes

½ cup walnuts, toasted

2 cups loosely packed fresh basil leaves

½ cup loosely packed fresh Italian parsley leaves

½ cup loosely packed fresh mint leaves

1 garlic clove, crushed and peeled

½ cup extra-virgin olive oil

Peperoncino flakes

2 small zucchini, cut into small dice (about 10 ounces)

1 pound spaghetti

½ cup freshly grated pecorino

Bring a large pot of salted water to a boil for the pasta. Put the cherry tomatoes, walnuts, basil, parsley, mint, and garlic in the work bowl of a food processor. Pulse to make a chunky paste. With the machine running, pour in the olive oil in a steady stream to make an almost smooth pesto. Season with salt and a big pinch of peperoncino. Scrape into a large serving bowl. Add the diced zucchini.

Meanwhile, add the spaghetti to the boiling water. When the pasta is al dente, remove it with tongs to the serving bowl with the sauce. Sprinkle with the grated cheese. Season with salt, if needed. Toss, adding up to ½ cup pasta-cooking water if it seems dry, to coat the pasta with the sauce, and serve.

Penne with Cauliflower and Green Olive Pesto

Penne con Cavolfiori e Pesto d'Olive Verdi

SERVES 6 • Cooking a vegetable along with the pasta, in this case cauliflower, is a great way to stretch a pound of pasta with healthy ingredients, without dirtying another pan. You could do the same here with broccoli or broccolini, green beans, or snap or snow peas.

Active Time: 20 minutes

Total Time: 20 minutes

Kosher salt

1 cup pitted Italian green olives, such as Castelvetrano

½ cup walnuts, toasted

2 cups loosely packed fresh Italian parsley leaves

2 garlic cloves, crushed and peeled

Peperoncino flakes

⅓ cup extra-virgin olive oil

1 pound penne

1 small cauliflower, cut or broken into small florets

½ cup freshly grated Grana Padano

Bring a large pot of salted water to a boil for the pasta. In the meantime, combine the olives, walnuts, parsley, garlic, and a large pinch of peperoncino in the work bowl of a mini–food processor. Pulse to make a chunky paste. With the machine running, add the olive oil in a steady stream to make a smooth pesto. Remove it to a serving bowl. Season with salt.

Add the penne to the boiling water. After about 2 minutes, add the cauliflower. When the pasta is al dente and the cauliflower is tender, remove them with a spider to the serving bowl with the sauce. Add the grated cheese; toss to coat the pasta with the sauce, adding up to ½ cup pasta-cooking water if it seems dry, and serve.

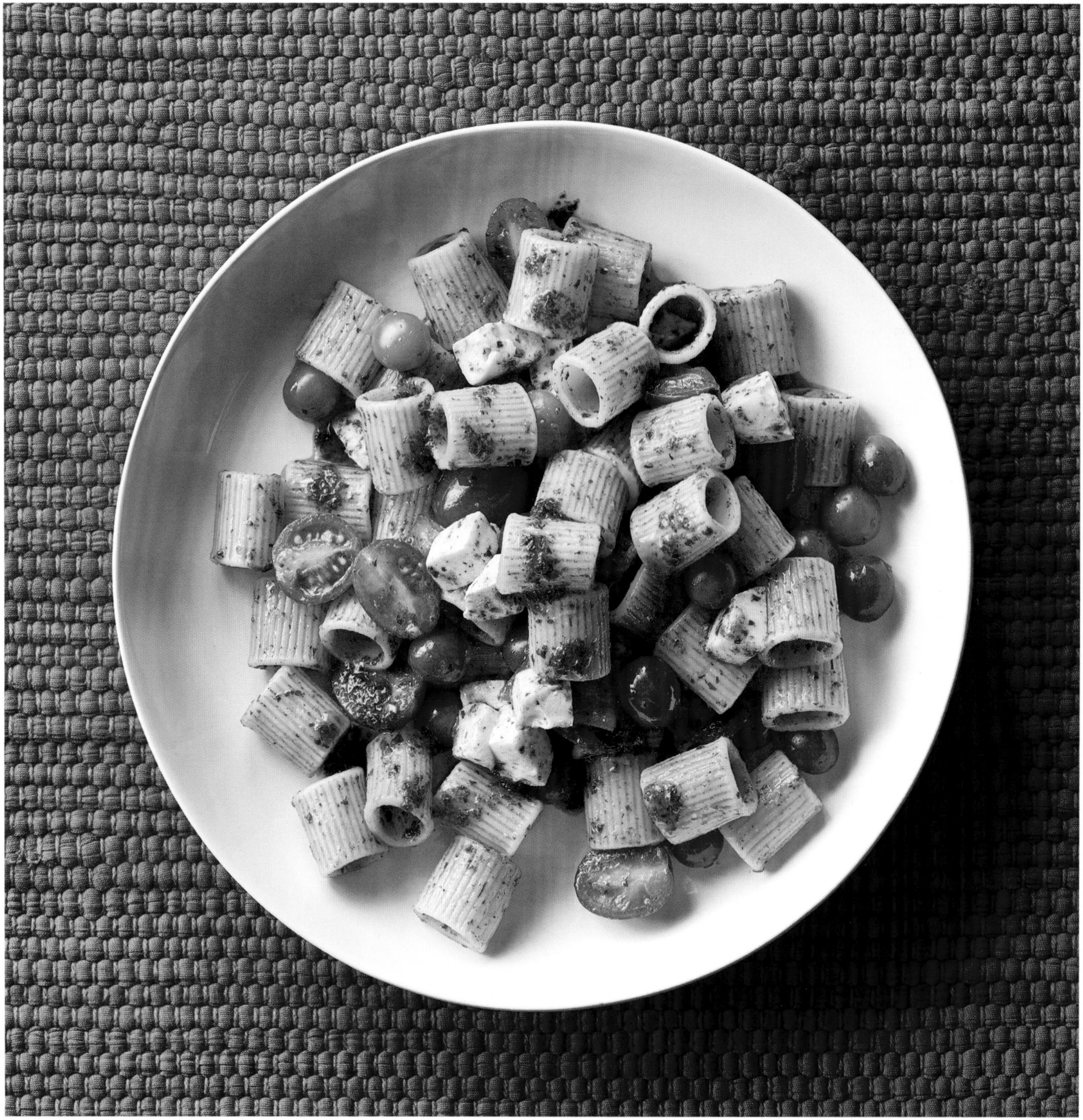

Mezzi Rigatoni with Raw Tomato Sauce

Mezzi Rigatoni al Pesto di Pomodoro Crudo

SERVES 6 · This is another recipe that is really just a starting point for your creativity and what you have on hand. You can use any type of tomatoes, as long as they are ripe and juicy—and at room temperature. You can also add other vegetables—some grated zucchini or a few handfuls of baby spinach or kale. Also feel free to toss in some protein, like leftover cooked shrimp, roast chicken, or pork, or a can of tuna. When you chop the tomatoes, make sure to scrape the juices from the cutting board into the serving bowl along with them—that'll be the flavor base for this easy, uncooked sauce.

Active Time: 25 minutes

Total Time: 25 minutes

Kosher salt

1 pint grape tomatoes, halved

Peperoncino flakes

1 pound mezzi rigatoni

1 cup loosely packed fresh basil leaves

½ cup loosely packed fresh Italian parsley leaves

2 garlic cloves, grated or finely chopped

⅓ cup extra-virgin olive oil

8 ounces fresh mozzarella, cut into ½-inch chunks

¾ cup freshly grated Grana Padano

Bring a large pot of salted water to a boil for the pasta. Chop tomatoes into ½-inch pieces, and add them and their juices to a serving bowl. Season with ½ teaspoon salt and ¼ teaspoon peperoncino. Toss, and let sit while you cook the pasta.

Add the pasta to the boiling water. Meanwhile, combine the basil, parsley, and garlic in the work bowl of a mini–food processor. Pulse to make a chunky paste. With the machine running, add the olive oil to make a smooth pesto. Add to the tomato mixture, and toss.

When the pasta is al dente, remove with a spider to the bowl with the tomatoes, and toss well. Add the mozzarella and grated Grana Padano, and toss well again. Season with salt if needed, toss again, and serve.

Fusilli with Salami and Roasted Peppers

Fusilli con Salame e Peperoni

SERVES 6 • Think of this as a warm pasta salad, which also makes for delicious leftovers at room temperature. If you are short on time, you can substitute good-quality jarred roasted peppers, but I think it's worth it to roast your own, since they're one of the stars of this dish. You can roast a big batch of five or six peppers at a time. Peel and slice them as I suggest below, and drizzle with olive oil. They'll keep in your refrigerator for a week or so, and you can enjoy them in pastas, frittatas, salads, and sandwiches.

Active Time: 30 minutes
Total Time: 30 minutes

Kosher salt

1 red bell pepper

1 yellow bell pepper

6 ounces thickly sliced Genoa salami, cut into matchsticks

4 ounces aged provolone, cubed

One 14-ounce can artichoke heart quarters, drained, coarsely chopped

6 tablespoons extra-virgin olive oil

1 pound fusilli

8 ounces green beans, trimmed and cut into 2-inch pieces

½ cup freshly grated Grana Padano

¼ cup chopped fresh Italian parsley

Freshly ground black pepper

Bring a large pot of salted water to a boil for the pasta. Set the peppers over the stovetop flame and char on all sides, about 4 minutes. (If you have an electric stove, you can char the peppers under the broiler.) Put them in a bowl, and cover tightly with plastic wrap. When they are cool, peel and slice the peppers.

Put the peppers in a large serving bowl with the salami, provolone, and artichokes. Drizzle with olive oil, and toss well. Let this mixture sit while you cook the pasta.

Add the fusilli to the boiling water. When the pasta is halfway cooked (in 4 or 5 minutes), add the green beans, and cook until the pasta is al dente. Remove with a spider to the serving bowl, and toss. Add the grated cheese and parsley, and season with salt and pepper. Toss and serve.

Capellini with Spicy Tomato Crab Sauce

Capellini con Sugo di Granchio Piccante

SERVES 6 • I am sometimes hesitant to write recipes using capellini, because it is so easy to overcook at home; however, it's the ideal choice here. I add a little extra liquid to the sauce, and the capellini cook in the sauce perfectly, absorbing the extra liquid and creating an elegant seafood-based pasta with lightning speed.

Active Time: 20 minutes

Total Time: 20 minutes

¼ cup extra-virgin olive oil, plus more for drizzling

4 garlic cloves, sliced

¼ to ½ teaspoon peperoncino flakes

One 28-ounce can San Marzano tomatoes, crushed by hand

Kosher salt

1 pound capellini

1 bunch scallions, green parts included, chopped

8 ounces crabmeat, picked over for shells

Heat a large skillet over medium-high heat. Add the olive oil. When the oil is hot, add the garlic. Once the garlic is sizzling, add the peperoncino. Add the tomatoes and 2 cups water. Simmer just until the sauce begins to come together, about 5 minutes. Season with 1 teaspoon salt.

Add the capellini, spreading it out and gently submerging it in the sauce. Cook and turn the capellini often until the pasta is al dente, 4 to 6 minutes (take care not to overcook; the pasta should still be quite chewy, and it will continue to cook off the heat). Mix in the scallions and crab, and simmer to heat through, stirring the capellini constantly. Finish with a drizzle of olive oil, toss, and serve immediately.

Skillet Lasagna

Lasagna in Padella

SERVES 4 • This is the dish to make when you're craving lasagna on a weeknight—it comes together in just 45 minutes! You can add additional vegetables to this if you like. Try browning some mushrooms—or, for heartier appetites, a few crumbled links of Italian sausages—in the olive oil before adding the sauce, or add a few handfuls of baby spinach to each layer.

Active Time: 20 minutes

Total Time: 45 minutes

Extra-virgin olive oil, for coating the skillet

3¼ cups marinara sauce (homemade or store-bought)

1 cup fresh ricotta

1 cup shredded low-moisture mozzarella

½ cup freshly grated Grana Padano

1 large egg, beaten

½ cup frozen peas

2 tablespoons chopped fresh Italian parsley

Kosher salt

Peperoncino flakes

12 sheets no-boil lasagna noodles

Heat a large nonstick skillet over medium heat. Add enough olive oil to make a thin film on the bottom of the skillet. Add 1¾ cups of the marinara with ¼ cup water, and bring to a simmer over medium heat.

In a bowl, combine the ricotta, ½ cup mozzarella, ¼ cup grated Grana Padano, the egg, peas, and parsley. Season with salt and a pinch of peperoncino, and mix well.

Layer three of the noodles in the skillet over the sauce. Dollop a third of the ricotta mixture on top of the pasta in the skillet, and spread it out to cover the noodles; then drizzle with ¼ cup of the tomato sauce. Make two more layers, ending with noodles. Drizzle with the remaining 1½ cups tomato sauce. Top with the remaining ½ cup mozzarella and ¼ cup grated cheese. Cover the skillet, and simmer until the pasta is al dente (test by piercing the center with a paring knife), 20 to 25 minutes. Preheat the broiler. Broil the lasagna just until the top is nicely browned, about 1 minute. Let it sit for 15 minutes before cutting and serving so the lasagna will settle and cut into portions more easily.

No-Boil Stuffed Shells

Conchiglie Ripiene al Forno

SERVES 4 TO 6 • This is another one of those dishes where you do not boil the pasta in advance, so you have to make sure there is enough liquid in the baking pan for the pasta to cook while in the oven. You can spoon the filling into the shells if you like, but the easiest and quickest thing to do is to put it in a quart-sized zip-top plastic bag (or piping bag). Press out the excess air, and snip a hole (one large enough for the shreds of cheese to come out without sticking) in one corner; then pipe the filling into the shells. This is a great dish to make when you have a crowd coming: you can multiply the recipe and make two or three baking dishes of it, as long as your oven can handle it.

Active Time: 15 minutes

Total Time: 1 hour 30 minutes

1 pound fresh ricotta

1 cup shredded low-moisture mozzarella

1 large egg, beaten

½ cup freshly grated Grana Padano

4 scallions, green parts included, chopped

¼ cup chopped fresh Italian parsley

Kosher salt

Freshly ground black pepper

3 cups marinara sauce (homemade or store-bought)

12 ounces jumbo pasta shells

Preheat the oven to 400 degrees. In a bowl, combine the ricotta, ½ cup of the mozzarella, the egg, ¼ cup of the Grana Padano, the scallions, and parsley. Season with salt and pepper.

Spread about 1 cup of the marinara in the bottom of a 9-by-13-inch baking dish. Fill the shells with the ricotta mixture (see headnote for instructions). Arrange in the baking dish. Stir together the remaining sauce and 1½ cups water. Spoon this over the shells. Cover with foil, and bake for 1 hour. Remove, and sprinkle with the remaining cheese. Bake, uncovered, until it's browned and bubbly, about 15 minutes more, and serve.

Summer Tomato and Basil Risotto with Mozzarella

Risotto con Pomodoro, Mozzarella, e Basilico

SERVES 4 TO 6 • You'll notice that this risotto starts with a little less hot liquid than my other recipes for the same amount of rice. That's because I want you to use ripe, juicy summer tomatoes and save as much of their juice as you can when you chop them. You'll also get extra liquid when you cook the tomatoes in the pan, creating a rich tomato flavor in a short amount of time.

Active Time: 40 minutes

Total Time: 40 minutes

2 tablespoons extra-virgin olive oil

3 shallots, chopped

1½ cups Arborio or other short-grain Italian rice

¾ cup dry white wine

1 pound ripe small tomatoes (such as Campari), quartered, juices reserved

Kosher salt

Peperoncino flakes

5 to 6 cups hot chicken broth, preferably homemade, or water

8 ounces fresh mozzarella, diced

½ cup loosely packed fresh basil leaves, chopped

½ cup freshly grated Grana Padano

1 tablespoon unsalted butter, cut into pieces

Heat the olive oil in a large skillet over medium heat. Add the shallots, and cook until they're softened, about 4 minutes. Add the rice, and stir to coat it in the oil. Cook and stir until the rice is translucent, about 2 minutes. Add the wine, and simmer until it's absorbed. Add the tomatoes and their juices, and keep on stirring until they begin to form a loose sauce, 1 to 2 minutes. Season with salt and peperoncino.

Add stock to cover, and cook until it's absorbed. Continue to stir, and add stock as it is absorbed until the rice is al dente. The process should take about 18 minutes from the first addition of liquid, with the final product still a bit loose, but not runny.

Stir in the mozzarella and basil. Remove the pan from the heat, and beat in the grated Grana Padano and butter. Serve immediately.

Mushroom and Sausage Risotto

Risotto con Funghi e Salsicce

SERVES 4 TO 6 • Use any combination of hearty mushrooms here—cremini, shiitake, oyster, and porcini are a good place to start. Avoid portobellos for this preparation, because their dark gills could muddy the color of the risotto.

Active Time: 40 minutes

Total Time: 40 minutes

2 tablespoons extra-virgin olive oil

12 ounces sweet Italian sausage, removed from casings

2 leeks, white and light-green parts, thinly sliced

1 teaspoon chopped fresh thyme leaves

1½ cups Arborio or other short-grain Italian rice

¾ cup dry white wine

8 ounces mixed wild mushrooms, thickly sliced

Kosher salt

Freshly ground black pepper

6 to 7 cups chicken broth, preferably homemade or low-sodium store-bought, or water

2 tablespoons unsalted butter, cut into pieces

½ cup freshly grated pecorino

Heat the olive oil in a large skillet over medium heat. Crumble in the sausage. Cook and crumble until it's browned, about 3 minutes. Remove to a plate. Add the leeks and thyme, and cook until the leeks are wilted, 3 to 4 minutes. Add the rice, and stir to coat it in the fat. Cook until the rice grains are translucent, about 2 minutes. Add the wine, and cook until it's absorbed. Stir in the mushrooms, and let them wilt a minute. Season with salt and pepper.

Add back the sausage, add stock to cover, and cook until it's absorbed. Continue to stir and add stock as it is absorbed until the rice is al dente. The process should take about 18 minutes from the first addition of liquid, with the final product still a bit loose, but not runny.

Off heat, beat in the butter and grated cheese. Serve immediately.

Seafood and Leek Risotto

Risotto di Mare con Porri

SERVES 4 TO 6 • *Risotto di mare* means risotto of the sea, and here I use shrimps and scallops, but as its name suggests, it can be made with any fish of your preference. It could be made with clams and mussels, or firm fish like monkfish. The rule to observe is cooking time. Clams and mussels take about 8 to 10 minutes to open up and cook, while monkfish takes about 15 minutes. When cooking fish, it is important not to overcook it, so keep this in mind if you choose to vary the kind of fish.

Active Time: 40 minutes

Total Time: 40 minutes

½ teaspoon saffron threads

6 to 7 cups hot water

3 tablespoons extra-virgin olive oil

2 leeks, white and light-green parts, thinly sliced

1 small onion, finely chopped

1 small fennel bulb, trimmed, cored, and finely chopped, plus ½ cup chopped tender fronds

1½ cups Arborio or other short-grain Italian rice

¾ cup dry white wine

Kosher salt

8 ounces medium-sized shrimp, peeled, deveined, tails removed, shrimp halved lengthwise

8 ounces sea scallops, side muscle or "foot" removed, scallops halved vertically if large

¼ cup chopped fresh Italian parsley

2 tablespoons unsalted butter, cut into pieces

Put the saffron in a measuring cup, and ladle over it 1 cup hot water. Let it steep while you begin the risotto.

Heat the olive oil in a large skillet over medium heat. Add the leeks, onion, and fennel, and cook until softened, about 5 minutes. Add the rice, and stir to coat it in the oil. Cook until the rice grains are translucent, about 2 minutes. Add the wine, and cook until it's absorbed. Add the saffron and soaking liquid and enough additional hot water to cover the rice, and cook until it's absorbed. Season with salt to taste. Continue to stir and add stock as it is absorbed until the rice is al dente, adding the shrimp and scallops when the rice is 4 to 5 minutes from being ready. The process should take about 18 minutes from the first addition of liquid, with the final product still a bit loose, but not runny.

Off heat, beat in the parsley, butter, and reserved fennel fronds, and serve.

Zucchini, Peas, and Pancetta Risotto

Risotto con Zucchine, Piselli, e Pancetta

SERVES 4 TO 6 • You can leave out the pancetta for a vegetarian version of this risotto. It is lovely with fresh shelled spring peas, but add them with the first or second addition of liquid, because they require longer cooking time than frozen ones. If you're making this in the summer, a handful of shredded zucchini flowers tossed in at the end would be delicious as well.

Active Time: 40 minutes

Total Time: 40 minutes

2 tablespoons extra-virgin olive oil

2 ounces pancetta, diced

1 medium onion, chopped

1½ cups Arborio or other short-grain Italian rice

¾ cup dry white wine

3 small zucchini, chopped (about 1 pound)

Kosher salt

Freshly ground black pepper

6 to 7 cups hot chicken broth, preferably homemade or low-sodium store-bought, or water

1 cup frozen peas, thawed

¼ cup chopped fresh chives

2 tablespoons unsalted butter, cut into pieces

½ cup freshly grated Grana Padano

Heat the olive oil in a large skillet over medium heat. Add the pancetta, and cook until it's just crisp, about 3 minutes. Add the onion, and cook until it's wilted, 3 to 4 minutes. Add the rice, and stir to coat it in the fat. Cook until the rice grains are translucent, about 2 minutes. Add the white wine, and cook until it's absorbed. Stir in the zucchini, and season with salt and pepper.

Add stock or water to cover, cook until it's absorbed, and give the rice a good mix. Continue to add stock and mix as the stock is absorbed until the rice is al dente, adding the peas for the last 5 minutes. The process should take about 18 minutes from the first addition of liquid, with the final product still a bit loose, but not runny.

Off heat, stir in the chives. Beat in the butter and grated cheese, and serve immediately.

Oat Risotto

Risotto d'Avena ai Funghi Porcini

SERVES 4 TO 6 • Oats make a hearty, nutty risotto with a toothsome texture. Be sure to use steel-cut oats here—old-fashioned oats are great for oatmeal, but won't give you the chew you want for this dish. If you can't find sunchokes, you can omit them or substitute another vegetable (sliced mushrooms work particularly well here).

Active Time: 35 minutes
Total Time: 50 minutes

2 tablespoons crumbled dried porcini
8 cups hot water
1 small onion, coarsely chopped
1 small carrot, coarsely chopped
1 stalk celery, coarsely chopped
2 garlic cloves, crushed and peeled
¼ cup extra-virgin olive oil
2 tablespoons tomato paste
2 cups steel-cut oats
Kosher salt
Freshly ground black pepper
2 fresh bay leaves
12 ounces sunchokes, peeled and sliced
2 cups diced peeled butternut squash (from about ½ small squash)
1 cup freshly grated Italian fontina
½ cup freshly grated Grana Padano

Put the porcini in a spouted measuring cup, and pour 1 cup of the hot water over them. Let them soften for about 5 minutes. Drain, reserving the soaking liquid, and finely chop the porcini.

Combine the onion, carrot, celery, and garlic in the work bowl of a food processor, and pulse to make an almost smooth *pestata*. Heat the olive oil in a large Dutch oven over medium heat. When the oil is hot, add the *pestata*. Cook and stir until it dries out and begins to stick to the bottom of the pot, 4 to 5 minutes.

Add the tomato paste and chopped porcini, and stir these into the *pestata*. Add the oats and stir while they toast for a minute or two. Season with salt and pepper. Pour in the remaining 7 cups of hot water and the reserved porcini liquid. Stir in the bay leaves. Bring to a rapid simmer, stirring occasionally. After 5 minutes, stir in the sunchokes and squash. Simmer until the vegetables are tender and the oats are cooked, but still have a bit of a chew to them, 20 to 25 minutes. Stir in the fontina and Grana Padano, remove the bay leaves, and serve.

Barley and Chicken Risotto

Risotto di Farro con Pollo

SERVES 4 TO 6 • I call for barley here, but you should feel free to think outside the box when making this or any risotto. You can use all sorts of grains as your base—wild rice, farro, kasha, or quinoa would all work well. Simply adjust the amount of liquid you use based on the package instructions for 2 cups of the grain.

Active Time: 30 minutes

Total Time: 1 hour 10 minutes

1 small onion, coarsely chopped

1 small carrot, coarsely chopped

1 stalk celery, coarsely chopped

¼ cup extra-virgin olive oil

1¼ pounds boneless, skinless chicken thighs, trimmed of excess fat and cut into 1-inch cubes

Kosher salt

Freshly ground black pepper

2 cups pearled barley, rinsed and drained

1 cup dry white wine

8 cups hot chicken stock, homemade or low-sodium store-bought

1 red bell pepper, diced

1 yellow bell pepper, diced

½ cup freshly grated Grana Padano

¼ cup chopped fresh Italian parsley

Combine the onion, carrot, and celery in the work bowl of a food processor, and pulse to make an almost smooth *pestata*.

Heat the olive oil in a large Dutch oven over medium heat. Season the chicken with salt and pepper. Brown the chicken pieces on all sides, about 4 minutes, and remove them to a plate.

Add the *pestata* to the pot. Cook and stir until it dries out and begins to stick to the bottom of the pot, 4 to 5 minutes. Return the chicken to the pot, and add the barley, stirring to coat it in the oil. Add the wine, and cook until it's absorbed, about 2 minutes. Add the stock, and adjust the heat so the mixture is simmering. Cover, and cook for 20 minutes.

Uncover, stir, and continue to cook until the barley is cooked but still a bit chewy, 15 to 20 minutes more, stirring in the peppers for the last 10 minutes.

Remove the barley from the heat, stir in the grated cheese and parsley, and serve.

Chicken and Rice

Riso con Pollo

SERVES 4 TO 6 • This is a more streamlined version of a traditional risotto. All of the stock is added at once and simmered. The result is a bit thicker and heartier than most risottos, and is sure to please the whole family. If you have leftover roasted or steamed vegetables (such as root vegetables, broccoli, or cauliflower) on hand, you can stir them in near the end of the cooking time. You could also add some thawed frozen peas or a few handfuls of baby greens, like spinach or kale.

Active Time: 25 minutes
Total Time: 45 minutes

1 medium onion, chopped

2 medium carrots, chopped

2 stalks celery, chopped

2 garlic cloves, chopped

3 tablespoons extra-virgin olive oil

1½ pounds boneless, skinless chicken thighs, trimmed of excess fat and quartered

Kosher salt

Freshly ground black pepper

2 cups Arborio or other short-grain Italian rice

2 teaspoons chopped fresh rosemary

1 cup dry white wine

2 fresh bay leaves

5 cups hot chicken stock, preferably homemade or low-sodium store-bought

2 tablespoons unsalted butter, cut into pieces

½ cup freshly grated Grana Padano

¼ cup chopped fresh Italian parsley

Combine the onion, carrots, celery, and garlic in the work bowl of a food processor, and process to make a *pestata*.

Heat the olive oil in a medium Dutch oven over medium-high heat. Season the chicken with salt and pepper. Brown on all sides in the oil, and remove to a plate. Add the *pestata*, and cook until it dries out and begins to stick to the bottom of the pot, about 6 minutes.

Add the rice, and sprinkle with the rosemary. Stir to combine. Add the wine, and simmer until it's absorbed. Add back the chicken, drop in the bay leaves, and pour in the stock. Return it to a simmer, and cook, uncovered, stirring occasionally, until the rice is al dente and the chicken is tender, about 18 minutes. Take off the heat, and beat in the butter and cheese. Stir in the parsley, remove the bay leaves, and serve.

Risotto Cakes

Riso al Salto

SERVES 2 TO 3 • If you're lucky enough to have leftover risotto in the fridge, you can have this dinner on the table in no time. I add grated zucchini for color, but you can also leave it out, especially if you're starting with a vegetable-heavy risotto.

Active Time: 20 minutes

Total Time: 50 minutes

2 cups leftover risotto (I especially like the Zucchini, Peas, and Pancetta Risotto, page 93)

1 small zucchini, grated on the coarse holes of a box grater (but see headnote)

⅓ cup freshly grated Grana Padano or pecorino

1 large egg, beaten

2 tablespoons chopped fresh Italian parsley

¼ cup chopped fresh chives

About ¾ cup fine dry bread crumbs

Vegetable oil, for frying

Kosher salt

1 tablespoon red wine vinegar

1 teaspoon Dijon mustard

2 tablespoons extra-virgin olive oil

Freshly ground black pepper

6 cups mixed salad greens

In a large bowl, combine the leftover risotto with the zucchini, grated cheese, egg, parsley, and 2 tablespoons chives. Form into six 1-inch-thick patties, and let them chill for 30 minutes.

Spread the bread crumbs on a plate, and press the patties into the crumbs to coat. Heat about ½ inch of vegetable oil in a large nonstick skillet over medium heat. Fry the patties until they're heated through and crispy on the outside, about 2 minutes per side. Drain on a paper-towel-lined plate, and season with salt.

Whisk together the vinegar and mustard in a large bowl. Whisk in the olive oil to make a smooth dressing. Season with salt and pepper. Add the salad greens and remaining chives, and toss well.

Serve the salad with the warm risotto cakes.

Pan Pizza

Pizza in Padella

SERVES 4 TO 6 • If you're up for making pizza dough yourself, the recipe opposite will make enough for one pan pizza. If not, ask your local pizza shop if they'll sell you a few balls of dough. Otherwise, frozen pizza dough from the grocery store also works well.

Active Time: 15 minutes

Total Time: 35 minutes

4 tablespoons extra-virgin olive oil, plus more for drizzling

1¼ cups canned San Marzano tomatoes, crushed by hand

4 garlic cloves, crushed and peeled

1 teaspoon dried oregano, preferably Sicilian oregano on the branch

Kosher salt

Peperoncino flakes

2 pounds pizza dough, at room temperature (opposite)

1½ cups grated low-moisture mozzarella

¼ cup freshly grated Grana Padano

Toppings (optional) such as mushrooms, pepperoni, roasted peppers, thinly sliced prosciutto, or other family favorites

Fresh basil leaves

Preheat the oven to 500 degrees. Combine 2 tablespoons olive oil, the tomatoes, garlic, and oregano in a medium bowl. Season with 1 teaspoon salt and a big pinch of peperoncino, and let this sauce sit while you prep the dough.

Brush a half-sheet pan with the remaining 2 tablespoons of olive oil. Punch down the dough, and spread it in the pan all the way to the edges. (If the dough doesn't stretch easily, stretch it as far as you can, wait a few minutes for it to relax, and then stretch again—repeating until you get all the way to the edges.)

Remove and discard the garlic from the sauce. Spread the sauce almost to the edges of the dough. Sprinkle with the mozzarella and grated Grana Padano. Layer on toppings of your choice. Bake on the bottom rack of the oven until the cheese is browned and bubbly and the underside of the crust is crisp and deep golden, 15 to 20 minutes. Tear the basil and sprinkle it over the top, and serve.

Pizza Dough

MAKES 2 POUNDS, ENOUGH FOR 1 HALF-SHEET PAN PIZZA

Active Time: 20 minutes

Total Time: 1 hour 50 minutes

1 package active dry yeast (about 2¼ teaspoons)

Pinch of sugar

½ cup warm water (about 100 degrees)

4 cups all-purpose flour, plus more for the counter and as needed

Kosher salt

3 tablespoons extra-virgin olive oil, plus more to coat the bowl

Sprinkle the yeast and sugar over the warm water in a small bowl. Let it sit until foamy, about 5 minutes.

Combine the flour and 2 teaspoons salt in a large bowl (or in the bowl of an electric mixer fitted with the dough hook). Add the yeast mixture, 1½ cups cold water, and the olive oil. Stir to make a shaggy dough. Knead on a floured counter, adding flour as needed, until the dough is smooth and springy, about 10 minutes by hand or 5 in the mixer. Coat a large bowl with olive oil, and turn to coat the dough in the oil. Cover with plastic wrap, and let the dough rise until doubled in size, about 1½ hours. Punch down, and proceed with your pizza recipe.

Tomato and Zucchini Bread Lasagna

Lasagna di Pane con Pomodori e Zucchine

SERVES 8 • This makes a large lasagna, ideal for leftovers. You can vary the cheese (use any good melting cheese) and vegetables (just use ones that aren't too dense; I wouldn't use root vegetables, for example) here to suit what you have on hand. In fact, that's what this recipe is all about, using odds and ends you've got left over in your kitchen to make something hearty and delicious. To get nice clean slices, don't forget to let the lasagna rest before cutting. It will stay piping hot for at least 30 minutes out of the oven.

Active Time: 20 minutes

Total Time: 1 hour 40 minutes

Unsalted butter, for the baking dish

1¼ cups freshly grated Grana Padano

Twelve ½-inch-thick slices day-old country bread

3 cups grated low-moisture mozzarella

3 medium zucchini, very thinly sliced lengthwise (about 1 pound)

Kosher salt

Freshly ground black pepper

3 cups marinara sauce (homemade or store-bought)

4 ounces thinly sliced prosciutto cotto or other sliced ham

Preheat the oven to 400 degrees. Butter a 9-by-13-inch baking dish. Have all of your ingredients on the counter before you begin preparing the lasagna.

Sprinkle the bottom and sides of the baking dish with about ¼ cup Grana Padano. Fit half of the bread slices in the bottom of the dish in one layer, breaking them to fit if needed. Sprinkle with ¼ cup grated Grana Padano and 1 cup of the mozzarella. Lay over this half of the sliced zucchini (it's okay if the slices overlap a little), and season with salt and pepper.

Spread 1 cup marinara sauce over the zucchini. Sprinkle with ¼ cup Grana Padano. Add all of the prosciutto cotto or ham in one layer. Add the final layer of zucchini; then sprinkle with 1 cup mozzarella. Fit the final layer of bread over the top. Press down with your palms, to compress everything in the dish. Spread the remaining 2 cups sauce over the bread. Sprinkle the remaining 1 cup mozzarella and ½ cup Grana Padano over the top.

Cover the baking dish with foil, tenting it so it doesn't touch the cheese, and bake until the edges are bubbly, about 45 minutes. Uncover, and bake until the top is deep golden brown, 15 to 20 minutes more. Let it sit about 15 minutes before serving.

FISH AND SEAFOOD

Skillet Tuna with Eggplant and Zucchini in Puttanesca Sauce 107
Tonno in Padella con Melanzane e Zucchine in Salsa Puttanesca

Seared Tuna with Balsamic Onions and Arugula-and-Fennel Salad 108
Tonno Scottato con Cipolle al Balsamico ed Insalata di Rucola e Finocchio

Monkfish Brodetto with Cannellini 111
Rana Pescatrice in Brodetto con Cannellini

Skillet Shrimp with Asparagus 112
Gamberi in Padella con Asparagi

Warm Shrimp and Squash Ribbon Salad 114
Insalata Tiepida di Gamberi e Nastri di Zucchine

Braised Calamari with Olives and Peppers 115
Calamari Affogati con Olive e Peperoni

Grilled Calamari Salad 116
Insalata di Calamari Grigliati

Mixed Seafood Bake 117
Pesce Misto al Forno

Mussels, Sausage, and Potatoes in White Wine 119
Cozze, Salsicce, e Patate al Vino Bianco

Halibut with Saffron Fregola 120
Ippoglosso con Fregola allo Zafferano

Rollatini of Sole with Cherry Tomatoes 121
Rollatini di Sogliola con Pomodorini

Crispy Baked Cod and Brussels Sprouts 122
Baccalà al Forno con Cavoletti di Bruxelles

Roasted Mustard Salmon with Cabbage and Carrots 124
Salmone alla Senape al Forno con Verza e Carote

Matalotta-Style Mixed Fish Stew 125
Zuppa di Pesce alla Matalotta

I love cooking and eating fish. Born on the Adriatic coast, I found the sea not only a great place to frolic in the summer, but also a good source of food. I recall many a time going fishing with my uncle Emilio, the family fisherman. He would take me and my brother, Franco, along because he needed help to row slowly while he dropped or pulled up the traps or prepared the bait, and to watch the lines while he organized the boat; there were no fishing poles then. I still recall the thrill of the tugs on the line at my fingers, the resistance as I held on tight, and the excitement when my uncle would pull up the catch. And, of course, that was dinner for all of us, although the best and biggest of the fish he would sell to restaurants.

Whether the fish were big or little, they were delicious. When cooking fish, there are two things that truly matter: the fish must be fresh, and you must not overcook it. I always get asked how one identifies the freshness of a fish. Use your senses. Smell is number one, and if your nose is not happy, beware. Then look at the eyes. They should be bright, clean, and looking at you, not set deep in the eye sockets. Press the flesh of the fish with your finger—with gloves, of course. If the meat is firm, that is a good sign. If your fingers sink into the flesh, look for another fish. I must say, if you find a good source of fresh-frozen fish, that can be a good option as well.

Monkfish has only recently become popular in America, but I recall eating it often in Italy, and it has always been one of my favorites. It is an ugly fish, with a big head and a mouth that opens from one end of the head to the other, but what's appealing about it is that its tail has one central gelatinous bone—no small bones, as most other fish have. It is usually sold in fillets, deboned. The texture is firm, the meat is white, and it has a sweet taste. It is a fish that will not easily overcook, is perfect for brodetto or fish soups, and does not fall apart. It is also a fish that you can prepare ahead for your arriving guests and reheat when they are ready for dinner. I recall that, when my uncle caught one and brought it home, my aunt would quickly make dinner by salting it, slightly dredging it in flour, pan-frying it until it formed a golden crust, and sprinkling it with a little salt. It was like eating lobster, maybe even better. So, next time you go to the fish counter, ask for a fillet of monkfish and think of me.

Skillet Tuna with Eggplant and Zucchini in Puttanesca Sauce

Tonno in Padella con Melanzane e Zucchine in Salsa Puttanesca

SERVES 4 • This recipe calls for tuna steaks, which can be expensive. Secondary cuts of tuna, such as tuna belly, can be used with results that are just as delicious.

Active Time: 20 minutes

Total Time: 45 minutes

¼ cup extra-virgin olive oil

1 medium onion, chopped

5 anchovy fillets

¼ cup coarsely chopped pitted Italian black olives

¼ cup drained capers in brine

1 medium eggplant, cut into 1-inch cubes

2 medium zucchini, cut into 1-inch cubes

Kosher salt

Peperoncino flakes

1 teaspoon chopped fresh thyme leaves

One 28-ounce can whole San Marzano tomatoes, crushed by hand

1½ pounds fresh tuna steak, cut into 1½-inch cubes

2 tablespoons chopped fresh Italian parsley

Heat the olive oil in a large skillet over medium heat. Add the onion, and cook until it's wilted, 4 to 5 minutes. Add the anchovies, olives, and capers, and cook until the onion begins to sizzle and the anchovies begin to dissolve, about 1 minute. Add the eggplant and zucchini. Season with ½ teaspoon salt and a big pinch of peperoncino. Cook, stirring occasionally, until the vegetables are lightly browned, about 5 minutes. Sprinkle with the thyme. Add the tomatoes and 1 cup water. Bring to a rapid simmer. Partially cover with the lid, and simmer until the sauce thickens and the vegetables are tender, similar to the consistency of caponata, about 20 minutes.

Uncover the skillet, and stir in the tuna. Simmer until the tuna is just cooked through, 5 to 7 minutes. Stir in the parsley, and serve.

Seared Tuna with Balsamic Onions and Arugula-and-Fennel Salad

Tonno Scottato con Cipolle al Balsamico ed Insalata di Rucola e Finocchio

SERVES 4 • Think of the red onions in this recipe as a quick relish. You could serve them over just about any grilled or sautéed protein, and they are also great on a sandwich. The salad can be a base for almost any type of fish or seafood. Fish (especially tuna) cooks quickly, so searing it and then combining it with the salad or sauce at the last minute works well.

Active Time: 20 minutes

Total Time: 20 minutes

5 tablespoons extra-virgin olive oil

2 medium red onions, cut into ½-inch rings

Kosher salt

5 tablespoons balsamic vinegar

1 pound tuna steak, 1 inch thick

6 cups baby arugula

1 medium fennel bulb, trimmed, halved, cored, and thinly sliced, plus ¼ cup tender fronds

6 radishes, thinly sliced (about ½ cup)

Heat 2 tablespoons of the olive oil in a large nonstick skillet over medium heat. Add the red onions, and toss to coat them in the oil. Season with salt and pepper. Cook until they're golden but still crunchy, 4 to 5 minutes. Add ¼ cup (4 tablespoons) of the balsamic vinegar. Simmer until it's syrupy, about 2 minutes. Remove the mixture to a plate.

Rinse or wipe the skillet clean, and increase the heat to medium high. Season the tuna with salt and pepper. Brush the tuna with 1 tablespoon of the olive oil and sear until it's browned on both sides, about 2 minutes per side for medium. Remove to the plate with the onions.

Combine the arugula, fennel, fronds, and radishes in a large serving bowl. Drizzle with the remaining tablespoon of vinegar and 2 tablespoons of the olive oil. Season with salt and pepper, and toss well. Slice the tuna, as you would a steak, and layer it over the salad. Top with the warm onion rings, and serve.

Monkfish Brodetto with Cannellini

Rana Pescatrice in Brodetto con Cannellini

SERVES 4 • Monkfish is a good choice for stews, because it is very sturdy and won't fall apart, and it won't overcook as rapidly as some other types of fish. This dish can be made in advance and brought to temperature when your friends or family arrive at the table. If you'd like to add a vegetable, stir in a cup or so of frozen peas when you add the monkfish back in.

Active Time: 35 minutes

Total Time: 35 minutes

1½ pounds monkfish fillet

Kosher salt

Freshly ground black pepper

All-purpose flour, for dredging

Vegetable oil, for frying

3 tablespoons extra-virgin olive oil

1 large onion, finely chopped

2 tablespoons tomato paste

¼ cup red wine vinegar

Two 15-ounce cans cannellini beans, rinsed and drained

¼ cup chopped fresh Italian parsley (optional)

Remove the translucent outer membrane from the monkfish by lifting and stripping it off with a paring knife (it may have already been removed by your fishmonger). Cut the monkfish into 1½-inch chunks. Season with salt and pepper. Lightly dredge the monkfish in flour.

Heat a large Dutch oven over medium heat. Add about ½ inch vegetable oil. When the oil is hot (a piece of fish dipped in it will sizzle on contact), brown the monkfish all over, in batches. Remove to a paper-towel-lined plate as it browns.

Once all of the fish is out of the pot, carefully pour out the vegetable oil and wipe the pot clean. Add the olive oil and return the pot to the heat. When the oil is hot, add the onion. Cook, stirring occasionally, until the onion begins to soften, 4 to 5 minutes. Make a spot in the center of the pan, and add the tomato paste to it. Cook and stir the tomato paste in that spot until it darkens a shade or two, about 1 minute. Add the red wine vinegar and 2 cups water. Bring to a rapid simmer, and cook to reduce the liquid slightly and blend the flavors, about 5 minutes. Return the monkfish to the pot, and simmer until just cooked through, about 5 minutes more.

Add the cannellini beans, season with salt and pepper, and stir to combine. Simmer until the broth is slightly thickened, 2 to 3 minutes. Stir in the parsley, and serve.

Skillet Shrimp with Asparagus

Gamberi in Padella con Asparagi

SERVES 4 • I love serving things like these grilled shrimp over toasted bread. It's an easy starch to prepare and makes a great base to soak up all of the buttery juices. If asparagus is not in season, you could also prepare this recipe with green beans, or sturdy greens like Swiss chard or escarole. You can also substitute scallops or chunks of salmon for the shrimp.

Active Time: 25 minutes

Total Time: 25 minutes

2 tablespoons unsalted butter

3 tablespoons extra-virgin olive oil

2 bunches medium thickness asparagus, tough ends trimmed, lower thirds peeled, cut into 2-inch lengths

¼ cup sliced almonds

Kosher salt

Peperoncino flakes

4 large or 8 small slices grilled or toasted country bread, for serving

1 pound large shrimp, peeled and deveined

1 lemon, halved

Melt the butter in 2 tablespoons of the olive oil in a large skillet over medium heat. When the butter is melted, add the asparagus, and toss to coat it. Cover, and cook until the asparagus are bright green but still al dente, about 5 minutes.

Uncover, and scatter in the almonds. Cook and toss until they are lightly toasted, 2 to 3 minutes. Season with ½ teaspoon salt and a big pinch of peperoncino. Lay the bread slices on a platter. Spoon the asparagus and almonds over them.

Return the skillet to the heat, and increase the heat to medium high. Add the remaining tablespoon of olive oil. Add the shrimp, and season with ½ teaspoon salt and a pinch of peperoncino. Cook and toss until the shrimp are just cooked through, about 3 minutes. Squeeze the lemon over the shrimp, and toss. Spoon the shrimp and juices over the asparagus and toast, and serve.

Warm Shrimp and Squash Ribbon Salad

Insalata Tiepida di Gamberi e Nastri di Zucchine

SERVES 4 • You can slice the vegetables evenly and thinly and they'll cook quickly, or they can be served raw. I use a Japanese mandoline to slice the vegetables here. It's a great, and inexpensive, investment for vegetable prep.

Active Time: 25 minutes

Total Time: 25 minutes

3 tablespoons extra-virgin olive oil

4 garlic cloves, crushed and peeled

1 pound large shrimp, peeled and deveined

Kosher salt

Peperoncino flakes

1 medium red onion, sliced

2 tablespoons unsalted butter

¼ cup drained capers in brine

3 tablespoons freshly squeezed lemon juice

1 medium zucchini, sliced lengthwise into ribbons

1 medium yellow squash, sliced lengthwise into ribbons

4 cups loosely packed baby spinach

Heat 2 tablespoons of the olive oil in a large skillet over medium-high heat. Add the garlic, and let it sizzle for a few seconds before adding the shrimp. Season the shrimp with ½ teaspoon salt and a pinch of peperoncino. Cook and toss until the shrimp are just cooked through, 3 to 4 minutes. Remove them with tongs to a large serving bowl, and discard the garlic.

Set the skillet back over the heat and reduce it to medium. Add the red onion, and season with salt. Cook and toss until the edges are golden but still crunchy, about 3 minutes. Add to the bowl with the shrimp.

Return the skillet to medium heat once more. Add the remaining tablespoon of olive oil to the skillet along with the butter. When the butter is melted, add the capers and cook until they're sizzling. Add the lemon juice, bring to a simmer, and cook just until the sauce comes together. Season with salt and peperoncino. Pour the sauce over the shrimp and onion slices in the bowl.

Add the zucchini, yellow squash, and spinach. Toss to wilt the vegetables slightly, and serve.

Braised Calamari with Olives and Peppers

Calamari Affogati con Olive e Peperoni

SERVES 4 · Calamari is another great choice for quick one-pot meals. It cooks in just a few minutes, so take care and sear it quickly, to prevent it from becoming rubbery. For this preparation, make sure you rinse, then dry the calamari very thoroughly, so it will sear, rather than steam in the skillet. This is particularly good served with some crusty bread, but it is also delicious served over polenta or used to dress pasta. With 1 pound of spaghetti, you could stretch this meal to feed six to eight people.

Active Time: 30 minutes

Total Time: 30 minutes

1 pound medium calamari, tubes and tentacles, tubes cut into 1-inch rings

3 tablespoons extra-virgin olive oil

Kosher salt

1 medium onion, sliced

2 stalks celery, chopped

1 red bell pepper, sliced

1 yellow bell pepper, sliced

Peperoncino flakes

1 teaspoon dried oregano, preferably Sicilian oregano on the branch

½ cup oil-cured black olives, pitted

2 tablespoons chopped fresh Italian parsley

Toss the calamari in a medium bowl with 2 tablespoons of the olive oil. Season with ¼ teaspoon salt. Heat a large nonstick skillet over high heat. Add the calamari in one layer, and sear, tossing once, until just cooked through, 2 to 3 minutes. Remove it to a plate.

Reduce the heat to medium. Add the remaining tablespoon of olive oil. When the oil is hot, add the onion, celery, and bell peppers. Season with ½ teaspoon salt and a big pinch of peperoncino. Sprinkle with the oregano, and toss until the vegetables begin to wilt, about 3 minutes. Add the olives. Cover the skillet, and cook, tossing occasionally, until the vegetables are tender and golden, 10 to 15 minutes. Add the calamari and any juices from the plate. Cook just to heat through, 1 to 2 minutes. Sprinkle with the parsley, toss, and serve.

Grilled Calamari Salad

Insalata di Calamari Grigliati

SERVES 4 • Weighting the calamari with a skillet on the grill is a good way to give it a nice char and keep it from curling up as it cooks. Calamari is often sold previously frozen, and this can be watery, so make sure you pat it very dry before grilling. If the calamari is fresh and the skin has been left on in good condition, leave it that way: it brings extra color and taste to the salad.

Active Time: 30 minutes

Total Time: 60 minutes
(includes marinating time)

1 pound medium calamari, tubes and tentacles

7 tablespoons extra-virgin olive oil

2 garlic cloves, crushed and peeled

Kosher salt

Peperoncino flakes

1 large red onion, cut into ½-inch rings

4 ears corn, shucked

12 ounces small tomatoes (such as Campari), quartered

¼ cup loosely packed fresh basil leaves, chopped

3 tablespoons red wine vinegar

Toss the well-dried calamari in a large bowl with 2 tablespoons of the olive oil and the garlic. Season with ¼ teaspoon salt and a big pinch of peperoncino. Cover, and marinate in the refrigerator for at least 30 minutes or up to overnight.

Heat a grill or a two-burner grill pan to medium heat. Brush the onion rings and corn with 1 tablespoon of the olive oil, and season with salt. Grill, turning occasionally, until both are charred and the onion is tender, 4 to 5 minutes for the onion, 5 to 6 minutes for the corn. Remove to a cutting board to cool slightly.

Increase heat to medium high. Lay the calamari on the grill, and weight with a large, heavy skillet. Cook, turning once, until it's charred and just cooked through, about 5 minutes in all. Remove to the cutting board.

Cut the calamari bodies into thick rings. Add to a serving bowl with the tentacles. Add the red onions. Cut the corn kernels from the cob directly into the bowl. Add the tomatoes and basil. Season with salt and peperoncino. Drizzle with the remaining 4 tablespoons olive oil and the vinegar. Toss well, and serve.

Mixed Seafood Bake

Pesce Misto al Forno

SERVES 4 • Roasting the sausage and vegetables in the oven before adding the seafood allows them to caramelize and add deep flavor to the cooking liquid in a relatively short amount of time. Make sure you use a wooden spoon to stir frequently in the last few minutes of reducing, to scrape up all of the delicious bits on the bottom of the pan.

Active Time: 15 minutes

Total Time: 55 minutes

12 ounces kielbasa or other smoked sausage, cut into 1-inch chunks

1 large onion, cut into thick rings

1 pound tiny new potatoes

3 tablespoons extra-virgin olive oil, plus more for drizzling

Kosher salt

Freshly ground black pepper

1 cup dry white wine

12 littleneck clams, scrubbed

2 pounds mussels, scrubbed

2 tablespoons chopped fresh Italian parsley

Preheat the oven to 425 degrees. Toss the kielbasa, onion, and potatoes in a large roasting pan with the olive oil. Season with ½ teaspoon salt and several grinds of black pepper. Roast, tossing once halfway through, until the vegetables are browned and tender, 20 to 25 minutes.

Pour in the wine, and add the clams and mussels. Cover the roasting pan tightly with foil, and roast until the clams and mussels open up, 12 to 15 minutes. Discard any that do not open.

Put the roasting pan on the stove over high heat. Bring the liquid to a boil, and cook and stir to reduce it slightly, about 2 minutes. Sprinkle with the parsley, and drizzle with olive oil. Toss and serve. I love to accompany this with some crusty country bread on the side.

Mussels, Sausage, and Potatoes in White Wine

Cozze, Salsicce, e Patate al Vino Bianco

SERVES 4 • Mussels are an excellent choice for weeknight one-pot cooking. They're economical, cook very quickly, and bring a lot of flavor to any dish. Traditionally, wild mussels could be sold very dirty and with stringy beards that needed to be removed one by one. Cultivated mussels (Prince Edward Islands are the most readily available) are much cleaner, and the shells simply need a quick scrubbing before going into the pot. Just make sure the mussels are fresh—trust your nose.

Active Time: 30 minutes

Total Time: 30 minutes

¼ cup extra-virgin olive oil

1 pound Yukon Gold potatoes, peeled, cut into ½-inch chunks

12 ounces sweet Italian sausage, removed from casings

1 medium onion, chopped

Kosher salt

Peperoncino flakes

1½ cups dry white wine

2 teaspoons chopped fresh thyme leaves

2 pounds mussels, scrubbed

¼ cup chopped fresh Italian parsley

Heat the olive oil in a large Dutch oven over medium heat. When the oil is hot, add the potatoes, and toss to coat. Cook, stirring often, until the potatoes begin to crisp and brown, about 5 minutes. Crumble in the sausage. Cook, breaking up the sausage with a wooden spoon, until the sausage is well browned, about 5 minutes. Add the onion, and cook until it begins to wilt, 2 to 3 minutes. Season with ½ teaspoon salt and a big pinch of peperoncino.

Add the white wine and thyme, bring to a boil, and cook until reduced by half, about 2 minutes. Add the mussels, adjust the heat to simmering, and cover the pot. Cook until all of the mussels have opened, 4 to 5 minutes, discarding any that don't open. Season with salt if needed, and stir in the parsley. Set the whole pot on a coaster in the middle of the table with a serving spoon, and make sure you have one or two empty vessels on the table for the shells.

Halibut with Saffron Fregola

Ippoglosso con Fregola allo Zafferano

SERVES 4 • Fregola is a small, round pasta from Sardinia. It's made by hand and has a rustic exterior that absorbs sauce well. This preparation is somewhere between a stew and a thick soup, but you can also cook the fregola in boiling water, as you would other pastas. It's more readily available now in Italian specialty shops, but if you have trouble finding it, you could adapt this recipe with another small pasta shape, like orzo or ditalini. If halibut is not available, a nice piece of any firm white fish, or even salmon, would also be very good.

Active Time: 35 minutes

Total Time: 35 minutes

1 teaspoon saffron threads

4 cups hot chicken stock, preferably homemade or low-sodium store-bought

1¼ pounds skinless halibut fillet, cut into large chunks

Kosher salt

Freshly ground black pepper

3 tablespoons extra-virgin olive oil

1 bunch scallions, including green parts, chopped

2 tablespoons tomato paste

2 teaspoons chopped fresh thyme leaves

Peperoncino flakes

1 cup fregola

½ cup dry white wine

1 cup frozen peas, thawed

2 tablespoons chopped fresh Italian parsley

Steep the saffron in the hot stock for 5 minutes. Season the halibut with ½ teaspoon salt and several grinds of pepper. Heat a large skillet over medium-high heat, and add 2 tablespoons of the olive oil. Brown the halibut all over, 2 to 3 minutes, and remove it to a plate.

Add the remaining tablespoon of olive oil to the skillet. Add the scallions, and cook until they're just wilted, about 2 minutes. Clear a spot on the bottom of the skillet, and add the tomato paste, thyme, and a pinch of peperoncino. Cook and stir the tomato paste in that spot until it toasts and darkens a shade or two; then add the fregola. Stir to coat the fregola in the tomato paste, and add the white wine. Bring it to a simmer, and cook until the wine is absorbed, about 1 minute. Add the hot chicken stock with the saffron, and season with ½ teaspoon salt. Adjust the heat so the mixture is simmering gently. Cover, and cook until the fregola is cooked through but still has a bit of a bite to it—10 to 13 minutes, depending on brand and size—uncovering halfway through to add the peas.

Uncover, and add the halibut chunks on top. Cover, and simmer just to heat the halibut through and finish cooking it, about 2 minutes. Season with salt if needed. Sprinkle with the parsley, stir gently, and serve with the fregola as the base and the halibut on top.

Rollatini of Sole with Cherry Tomatoes

Rollatini di Sogliola con Pomodorini

SERVES 6 • This is one of those recipes that you can prepare in advance and keep in the refrigerator, ready to go into a hot oven when your guests arrive. Fillet of sole is ideal for this preparation, but if sole is not in season, a fillet of another white fish like fluke, halibut, or flounder could be substituted, just as long as it is not too flaky. If you have day- or two-day-old bread, pulse it in the food processor or grate it on the coarse holes of a box grater and use that instead of the bread crumbs. Just make sure the crumbs are adequately moistened with olive oil for the filling.

Active Time: 20 minutes

Total Time: 25 minutes

1½ cups fine dry bread crumbs

6 tablespoons extra-virgin olive oil

3 scallions, green parts included, chopped

1 lemon, zested, then halved and thinly sliced

¼ cup chopped fresh Italian parsley

1 teaspoon chopped fresh thyme leaves

Kosher salt

2 tablespoons unsalted butter, cut into pieces

3 garlic cloves, thinly sliced

1 cup dry white wine

Peperoncino flakes

6 sole fillets (about 6 to 7 ounces each)

1 pint halved cherry or grape tomatoes

Preheat the oven to 400 degrees. Combine the bread crumbs, 3 tablespoons of the olive oil, the scallions, grated lemon zest, 2 tablespoons of the parsley, and the thyme in a medium bowl. Season with ½ teaspoon salt, and toss to combine.

In a large baking dish (10-by-15-inch or similar), combine 2 tablespoons of the olive oil, the butter, garlic, lemon slices, white wine, the remaining 2 tablespoons parsley, and a pinch of peperoncino. Season with salt.

Lay the sole fillets on your work surface, with the sides where the skin was facing up. Brush with the remaining tablespoon of olive oil, and season with salt. Fill each with 3 to 4 tablespoons of the bread-crumb filling. Roll up the fillets, and set them, seam side down, in the baking dish. Scatter the tomatoes in the spaces between the fillets. Sprinkle any leftover bread-crumb mixture over the top. Bake until the fish is cooked through, the bread crumbs are crisp, and the tomatoes have broken down into a chunky sauce, about 25 minutes, and serve.

Crispy Baked Cod and Brussels Sprouts

Baccalà al Forno con Cavoletti di Bruxelles

SERVES 4 • The quick sauce of lemon, parsley, and oil that I drizzle over the cod and Brussels sprouts at the end is an easy way to brighten it up. This versatile sauce will add life to just about any cooked fish or seafood, and would also be great for roast chicken. The recipe is an easy one to multiply when you have more guests coming, but in that case do the vegetables and fish on separate baking sheets.

Active Time: 45 minutes

Total Time: 45 minutes

1¼ pounds Brussels sprouts, trimmed and halved

6 tablespoons extra-virgin olive oil, plus more for brushing

1 teaspoon sweet paprika

Kosher salt

Freshly ground black pepper

1 cup panko bread crumbs

Grated zest and juice of 1 lemon

¼ cup chopped fresh chives

½ teaspoon Old Bay seasoning

Four 6-ounce skinless cod fillets

2 tablespoons chopped fresh Italian parsley

Preheat the oven to 425 degrees. Toss the Brussels sprouts on a rimmed baking sheet with 2 tablespoons of the oil, the paprika, ½ teaspoon salt, and several grinds of black pepper. Roast them until they're lightly golden and crisp-tender, about 15 minutes.

Meanwhile, in a shallow bowl, combine the panko bread crumbs, lemon zest, chives, Old Bay, and ½ teaspoon salt. Brush the cod with olive oil, and season it with salt and pepper. Dip it into the bread crumbs, covering on all sides.

After the Brussels sprouts have been cooking about 15 minutes, push them to one side of the baking sheet to make room for the cod. Add the cod to the baking sheet, patting on more crumbs. Sprinkle the remaining crumbs over the sprouts. Roast until the cod is cooked through and the crumbs are crispy, 13 to 15 minutes.

In a small bowl, whisk together the remaining ¼ cup olive oil, the lemon juice, and parsley. Season with ¼ teaspoon salt and several grinds of pepper. Drizzle this sauce over the cod and Brussels sprouts before serving.

Roasted Mustard Salmon with Cabbage and Carrots

Salmone alla Senape al Forno con Verza e Carote

SERVES 4 • Salmon is a good fish for roasting, because it's firm and fatty and will hold its shape well. If you like your salmon on the rare side, cut the final roasting time back by a few minutes. This recipe will also work well with firm white fish.

Active Time: 10 minutes

Total Time: 45 minutes

½ cup cider vinegar

¼ cup grainy mustard

¼ cup extra-virgin olive oil, plus more for the baking sheet

1 tablespoon honey

2 teaspoons chopped fresh thyme leaves

Kosher salt

Freshly ground black pepper

1 small savoy cabbage, quartered and cored

2 large carrots, cut into 2-inch sticks

Four 6-to-8-ounce salmon fillets

Preheat the oven to 425 degrees. Whisk together the cider vinegar, mustard, olive oil, honey, and thyme in a spouted measuring cup. Season with 1 teaspoon salt and several grinds of black pepper.

Brush a large, rimmed baking sheet with olive oil. Spread the cabbage and carrots on the baking sheet. Brush them all over with about a third of the sauce. Roast until the vegetables are browned and almost tender, about 20 minutes, turning and brushing again with another third of the sauce halfway through.

Push the vegetables to one side of the baking sheet to make room for the salmon. Season the salmon lightly with salt and pepper. Brush the salmon with the remaining sauce, and add it to the baking sheet. Roast until the vegetables are tender and the salmon is cooked through, 15 to 18 minutes, and serve.

Matalotta-Style Mixed Fish Stew

Zuppa di Pesce alla Matalotta

SERVES 4 • You can (and should!) vary the seafood here based on what is good and fresh in your market, such as monkfish, striped bass, or halibut. For this preparation, I like littlenecks on the smaller side, but you could also use manila clams or even cockles—though double the number of cockles since they are so tiny. This dish becomes a whole meal with the simple addition of a loaf of crusty bread.

Active Time: 40 minutes

Total Time: 40 minutes

1 pound skinless grouper fillet, cut into 2-inch chunks

Kosher salt

All-purpose flour, for dredging

¼ cup extra-virgin olive oil, plus more for drizzling

1 medium onion, chopped

3 stalks celery, chopped

2 fresh bay leaves

1 cup dry white wine

¾ cup pitted large green olives, such as Cerignola, halved

3 tablespoons drained capers in brine

One 28-ounce can whole San Marzano tomatoes, crushed by hand

Peperoncino flakes

12 littleneck or other small clams

8 ounces large shrimp, peeled and deveined

Season the grouper with ¼ teaspoon salt. Spread the flour in a shallow bowl or plate. Lightly dredge the grouper in flour. Heat the olive oil in a large Dutch oven over medium heat. Brown the grouper all over, and remove it to a plate.

With the heat still at medium, add the onion and celery. Cook until the onion begins to wilt, about 5 minutes. Add the bay leaves and wine, and adjust the heat so the wine is simmering rapidly. Cook until it's reduced by half, about 2 minutes. Add the olives and capers, and let them sizzle a minute. Add the tomatoes, rinse the can out with 1 cup water, and add that. Season with ½ teaspoon salt and a big pinch of peperoncino. Simmer until the celery and onions are tender, about 15 minutes.

Stir in the clams. Cover and simmer until the clams begin to open, about 3 minutes. Stir in the shrimp, and gently settle the grouper in the sauce. Simmer until the shrimp and grouper are cooked through and all of the clams have opened (discard any that haven't), 3 to 4 minutes more. Discard the bay leaves. Season with salt, if needed, and drizzle with a little more olive oil before serving.

MEAT AND POULTRY

One-Pan Chicken and Eggplant Parmigiana 130
Pollo e Melanzane alla Parmigiana

Chicken and Brussels Sprouts 132
Pollo e Cavoletti di Bruxelles al Forno

Chicken Legs with Artichokes and Cider Vinegar 133
Cosce di Pollo con Carciofi all'Aceto di Mele

Skillet Chicken Thighs with
Cerignola Olives and Potatoes 135
Cosce di Pollo con Olive di Cerignola e Patate

Poached Chicken and Vegetables in Broth
with Green Sauce 136
Pollo Sobbollito con Verdure e Salsa Verde

Chicken Cacciatore 138
Pollo alla Cacciatora

Skillet Gratinate of Chicken, Mushrooms,
and Tomato 140
*Petto di Pollo Gratinato con Funghi
e Pomodoro*

Roast Turkey Breast with Dried Fruit
and Root Vegetables 141
Petto di Tacchino Arrosto con Frutta Secca e Tuberi

Skillet Gratinate of Pork, Eggplant, and Zucchini 143
Filetto di Maiale con Melanzane e Zucchine Gratinati

Spicy Sheet Pan Pork Chops and Broccoli 144
Braciole di Maiale Piccanti al Forno con Broccoli

Skillet Ricotta Mini–Meat Loaves 145
Mini Polpettoni con Ricotta

Cheesy Veal Chops with Cabbage 146
Costolette di Vitello Farcite di Fontina con Verza

Skillet Sausages with Fennel and Apples 147
Salsicce in Padella con Finocchio e Mele

Skillet Sausage and Peppers 148
Salsicce e Peperoni in Padella

Lamb and Winter Squash Stew 151
Spezzatino d'Agnello con Zucca

London Broil with Peppers and Onion 152
London Broil con Peperoni e Cipolla

Mozzarella Cheeseburgers 153
Cheeseburgers con Mozzarella

Beer-Braised Beef Short Ribs 154
Costolette di Manzo Brasate alla Birra

Chicken Scaloppine in Lemon Caper Sauce
with Spinach 156
Petto di Pollo al Limone e Capperi con Spinaci

Beef Goulash 157
Goulash di Manzo

Pork Guazzetto with Beans 158
Guazzetto di Maiale con Fagioli

Balsamic Chicken Stir-Fry 159
Bocconcini di Pollo in Padella al Balsamico con Broccoli

Italians are not reared on grilled steaks; braising, roasting, stewing, and boiling are techniques often used at home. Not only does combining meat with herbs, spices, and vegetables yield a complex and delicious dish, like Chicken Cacciatore (page 138), Chicken Legs with Artichokes and Cider Vinegar (page 133), Lamb and Winter Squash Stew (page 151), Beef Goulash (page 157), and Pork Guazzetto with Beans (page 158), but some of these cooking techniques allow us to use secondary cuts of the animal, which benefit from longer cooking time, without wasting anything. Today it is in vogue for chefs to cook snout to tail, but I recall that my grandma often cooked tripe, oxtails, lambs' necks, pigs' ears, and chicken liver, and she even made blood sausages when it was slaughter time.

The recipes in this chapter are ideal for a one-pot meal, and in them meat goes a long way when combined with vegetables, as in Spicy Sheet Pan Pork Chops and Broccoli (page 144), Cheesy Veal Chops with Cabbage (page 146), and Skillet Sausages with Fennel and Apples (page 147). This is a healthier way to eat. Instead of a meal that is 75 percent protein, let's make it 40 or 50 percent protein, and make the rest vegetables, legumes, and starches. Also, most of these recipes can be made in advance, portioned and frozen, then reheated when needed.

And, of course, the beauty of these dishes is that you do not have to worry about a side dish or balancing a meal—everything is in one pot, in one recipe.

One-Pan Chicken and Eggplant Parmigiana

Pollo e Melanzane alla Parmigiana

SERVES 4 • This is chicken-and-eggplant parmigiana all cooked and layered in one skillet. I brown both ingredients in olive oil, but skip the breading, which saves time and is healthier, and then proceed to make the sauce, top with cheese, and—done! Quick and delicious.

Active Time: 30 minutes

Total Time: 55 minutes

1 medium Italian eggplant (about 12 ounces)

Kosher salt

1½ pounds thinly sliced on a bias, boneless, skinless chicken breast (about 12 pieces)

All-purpose flour, for dredging

Extra-virgin olive oil, as needed

4 garlic cloves, crushed and peeled

One 28-ounce can San Marzano tomatoes, crushed by hand

Peperoncino flakes

¼ cup chopped fresh basil leaves

1½ cups grated low-moisture mozzarella

½ cup freshly grated Grana Padano

Preheat the oven to 425 degrees. Remove vertical stripes of peel from the eggplant with a vegetable peeler. Slice the eggplant crosswise on the bias into ¼-inch-thick slices, ideally about twelve in total. Season with ½ teaspoon salt. Season the chicken pieces with 1 teaspoon salt. Spread the flour in a shallow bowl, and lightly dredge the eggplant and the chicken.

Heat a large nonstick skillet over medium-high heat. Add a thin film of olive oil. Brown the eggplant in batches, 2 or 3 minutes per batch, removing them to a plate as they brown. Add more oil, if needed. Brown the chicken in batches, 2 to 3 minutes per batch, removing the pieces to the same plate as the eggplant (if they will fit) as they brown. Discard the oil, and wipe the pan clean with a paper towel.

Return the skillet to medium heat. Add 3 tablespoons of olive oil. When the oil is hot, add the garlic, and cook until it's sizzling, about 1 minute. Add the tomatoes and ½ cup water. Season with ½ teaspoon salt and a large pinch of peperoncino. Simmer until the sauce thickens slightly, 8 to 10 minutes. Stir in the basil.

Shingle the chicken and eggplant in the skillet, alternating them, starting around the edge of the pan and then filling in the middle. Sprinkle with the cheeses. Bake until browned and bubbly all over, 20 to 25 minutes, and serve.

Chicken and Brussels Sprouts

Pollo e Cavoletti di Bruxelles al Forno

SERVES 4 • If Brussels sprouts are out of season, this dish is just as delicious with potatoes, butternut squash, or whole button mushrooms. They only need to be peeled, cleaned, and cut into 1-inch cubes. Use this recipe as a template and substitute with other vegetables, always keeping in mind that cooking time can vary by vegetable, and adding them to the chicken in the roasting pan accordingly. I also make it with only drumsticks or wings, and it would be delicious with baby back spareribs cut individually. Just keep in mind that ribs take a little longer to cook.

Active Time: 20 minutes

Total Time: 1 hour 35 minutes

1 whole chicken (3 pounds), cut up, or 3 pounds chicken parts

Kosher salt

5 tablespoons extra-virgin olive oil

3 small onions, peeled and quartered through the root end

1 pound Brussels sprouts, trimmed and halved

8 garlic cloves, crushed and peeled

2 sprigs fresh rosemary

4 ounces slab bacon, cut into lardons

½ cup dry white wine

Preheat the oven to 425 degrees. Season the chicken with 1 teaspoon salt, and rub with 2 tablespoons of the olive oil. Spread on a large, rimmed baking sheet, skin side up. Toss the onions, Brussels sprouts, and garlic in a large bowl with the remaining 3 tablespoons olive oil. Season with ½ teaspoon salt. Spread on the baking sheet with the chicken.

Tear the rosemary sprigs over the chicken and vegetables, and scatter the bacon pieces over as well. Pour the wine into the pan. Roast, tossing once but leaving the chicken skin side up, until the wine is reduced and the chicken skin is crisp, 1 hour to 1 hour 15 minutes.

Chicken Legs with Artichokes and Cider Vinegar

Cosce di Pollo con Carciofi all'Aceto di Mele

SERVES 4 • I was inspired to create this dish with leftovers from recipe testing. We had some extra artichokes cleaned and with their hearts quartered. I popped them into the freezer, and found them to create this dish for Grandma and me for dinner one night. You can use packaged frozen artichoke hearts, or four large fresh artichokes you've cleaned and quartered yourself. There are a lot of chicken breast recipes out there, but I like the thigh and drumstick of the chicken the best and am always looking for ways to prepare them.

Active Time: 1 hour
Total Time: 1 hour

4 whole chicken legs, separated at the joint (about 2 pounds)

Kosher salt

2 tablespoons extra-virgin olive oil

6 garlic cloves, crushed and peeled

8 small onions, such as cipollini, cleaned and peeled but left whole

One 9-ounce package frozen artichoke hearts, thawed

Peperoncino flakes

2 sprigs fresh rosemary

½ cup apple-cider vinegar

Season the chicken with 1 teaspoon salt. Heat the olive oil in a large non-stick skillet over medium heat. Brown the chicken pieces until they're golden on both sides, 6 to 7 minutes. Nestle the garlic and onions in the spaces between the pieces of chicken. Cook until they begin to caramelize, about 5 minutes.

Nestle the artichoke pieces in the pan. Shake the pan, tossing to combine the ingredients and circulate the juices in the bottom. Season with salt and peperoncino. Break the rosemary sprigs into a few pieces, and add them to the pan. Cover the skillet, and reduce the heat so the chicken browns slowly. Cook, tossing everything occasionally, until the chicken and vegetables are deep golden brown, about 15 minutes.

Raise the heat to high, and add the vinegar and ½ cup water, put the lid back on, and lower the flame so the liquid is simmering. Cook until the chicken is tender, about 15 minutes more. Uncover, increase the heat to medium, and let the liquid reduce, tossing everything occasionally, until the sauce has thickened and the chicken and vegetables are lightly glazed, 5 to 7 minutes. Remove rosemary sprigs, and serve.

Skillet Chicken Thighs with Cerignola Olives and Potatoes

Cosce di Pollo con Olive di Cerignola e Patate

SERVES 4 • Chicken thighs are a wonderful cut for one-pot braising. They're flavorful and juicy, but also very forgiving. A few extra minutes in the pan is not a big deal, because they're difficult to overcook. Cerignola are large and meaty green olives with a mild flavor, making them perfect for a preparation like this, although you can use any large green olive here. If they're very salty or briny, give them a quick rinse before adding them to the skillet.

Active Time: 1 hour

Total Time: 1 hour

8 bone-in, skin-on chicken thighs (about 2½ pounds)

Kosher salt

Freshly ground black pepper

3 tablespoons extra-virgin olive oil

1½ pounds Yukon Gold potatoes, cut into 1-inch chunks

2 medium red onions, cut into 6 wedges each, left attached at the root end

2 sprigs fresh sage

¼ cup white wine vinegar

¾ cup crushed and pitted Cerignola olives

¼ cup chopped fresh Italian parsley

Season the chicken thighs with 1 teaspoon salt and several grinds of pepper. Heat the olive oil in a large skillet or shallow Dutch oven over medium heat. Brown the chicken on both sides, 8 to 10 minutes in all. What is important when cooking chicken thighs with the skin on is that you get the skin crisp, so cook on all sides until it is. Remove chicken thighs to a plate as they brown.

Add the potatoes to the skillet, and toss to coat them in the oil. Season with salt and pepper. Cook and toss until the potatoes are golden. As with the chicken, you want the potatoes to get nice and golden brown, in 7 to 10 minutes. Add the onions, lower the heat, and cover the skillet. Cook until the onions begin to wilt, about 3 minutes. Uncover, and add the sage and vinegar. Cover, and simmer 15 minutes.

Uncover, stir up the crusty bits at the bottom of the skillet, and add ½ cup water. Stir in the olives. Cover the skillet, and cook until the chicken is tender, about 20 minutes more. Uncover, and increase the heat to reduce the sauce slightly, 3 to 4 minutes. Sprinkle with the parsley, and serve.

Poached Chicken and Vegetables in Broth with Green Sauce

Pollo Sobbollito con Verdure e Salsa Verde

SERVES 4 • You can serve the chicken with green sauce, which will make a great meal in itself, reserving the broth for another meal, or you can serve this dish with the broth, having the carrots as an appetizer or on the side of the chicken with the green sauce. If you want to use the broth for a separate meal, combine it with any leftover vegetables and some rice and pasta to make a quick soup. When I was a child, we would also have a rich broth like this over toasted bread cubes for a filling soup made out of almost nothing.

Active Time: 30 minutes

Total Time: 2 hours 15 minutes

Chicken

Handful of fresh Italian parsley sprigs, plus chopped parsley for garnish

4 fresh bay leaves

One 2-by-2-inch piece Grana Padano rind, scraped clean

2 garlic cloves, crushed and peeled

1 teaspoon black peppercorns

2 strips lemon peel, removed with a peeler

Kosher salt

1 large roasting chicken (about 3 to 3½ pounds)

3 leeks, white and light-green parts, trimmed but left whole

2 large carrots, peeled and halved crosswise

2 stalks celery, halved crosswise

4 small turnips, peeled but left whole

For the chicken, bring 4 quarts water to a simmer in a large pot or medium Dutch oven. Add the parsley, bay leaves, cheese rind, garlic, peppercorns, and lemon peel. Season with 1 teaspoon salt. Return to a simmer to blend the flavors, and cook about 15 minutes.

Add the chicken, leeks, carrots, celery, and turnips. Return to a simmer, and cook until chicken and vegetables are very tender, 1 hour 15 minutes to 1½ hours. Strain and reserve the broth, but keep it warm. Set the chicken and vegetables aside, discarding the bay leaves.

For the sauce, combine the parsley, lemon juice, cornichons, and horse-radish in the work bowl of a mini–food processor. Pulse until chunky. With the machine running, add the olive oil to make a smooth dressing. Season with salt and peperoncino.

To serve, tear the chicken meat into chunks, discarding the skin and bones. Cut the vegetables into large chunks. Put the chicken and vegetables on a platter, and drizzle with a little of the sauce, serving the rest on

Sauce

2 cups fresh Italian parsley leaves

¼ cup freshly squeezed lemon juice

8 cornichons

1 tablespoon drained prepared horseradish

¾ cup extra-virgin olive oil

Kosher salt

Peperoncino flakes

the side. Make sure the broth is warm before serving. Serve a bowl of hot broth and some grated Grana Padano, and the diners can add chicken and vegetables to the broth or have the broth first, then the chicken and vegetables with sauce as a second course.

Chicken Cacciatore

Pollo alla Cacciatora

SERVES 4 • You could also use either a whole cut-up chicken or a combination of drumsticks and thighs here. If you have leftovers, strip the chicken meat from the bones and add it back to the sauce. It makes a nice pasta dressing, with the addition of a little pasta-cooking water, a drizzle of olive oil, and some grated Grana Padano. I like Chicken Cacciatore served with polenta, as it is traditionally eaten by game hunters. I recall that, when my grandfather brought home a pheasant, hare, or boar, Grandma would always prepare a big pot of polenta to go with it.

Active Time: 30 minutes

Total Time: 1 hour 15 minutes

8 chicken drumsticks
(about 2½ pounds)

Kosher salt

3 tablespoons extra-virgin olive oil

1 sweet onion, thickly sliced

1 yellow bell pepper, thickly sliced

8 ounces cremini mushrooms, quartered

½ cup dry white wine

One 28-ounce can whole San Marzano tomatoes, crushed by hand

1 teaspoon dried oregano, preferably Sicilian oregano on the branch

Peperoncino flakes

2 tablespoons chopped fresh Italian parsley (optional)

Season the chicken with ½ teaspoon salt. Heat the oil in a large Dutch oven over medium heat. Brown the chicken on all sides, 7 to 8 minutes, and remove it to a plate. Add the onion and pepper, and cook until they begin to wilt, 6 to 7 minutes. Add the mushrooms, and cook until they begin to soften, about 3 minutes. Season the vegetables with salt.

Add the wine, and simmer until it's reduced by half, about 2 minutes. Add the tomatoes and 1 cup water. Return the chicken to the pot. Add the oregano, and season with 1 teaspoon salt and a big pinch of peperoncino. Simmer, uncovered, until the sauce has thickened and the chicken is tender, about 45 minutes, stirring once or twice throughout the cooking process. Stir in the parsley, and serve.

Skillet Gratinate of Chicken, Mushrooms, and Tomato

Petto di Pollo Gratinato con Funghi e Pomodoro

SERVES 4 • I always encourage you to make my recipes your own, so consider this recipe as a jumping-off point. Use any thinly sliced protein you like: pork loin, veal scaloppine, or turkey cutlets would all work. If you'd like a nice browned top, run the skillet under the broiler for a moment before serving.

Active Time: 40 minutes

Total Time: 40 minutes

4 tablespoons unsalted butter

1 tablespoon extra-virgin olive oil

8 shiitake mushrooms, stems removed

All-purpose flour, for dredging

2 large boneless, skinless chicken breasts, halved crosswise/butterflied (about 1½ pounds)

Kosher salt

Freshly ground black pepper

1 firm medium-sized beefsteak tomato (about 1 pound), 4 slices, remainder chopped and reserved for the sauce

4 large fresh sage leaves

½ cup dry white wine

1 cup chicken broth, preferably homemade or low-sodium store-bought

¾ cup freshly grated Italian fontina

¼ cup freshly grated Grana Padano or pecorino

2 tablespoons chopped fresh Italian parsley

Melt 2 tablespoons of the butter in the olive oil in a large skillet over medium heat. Add the mushroom caps, and brown on both sides, 1 to 2 minutes per side. Remove them to a plate.

Spread the flour in a shallow bowl or plate. Season the chicken with ½ teaspoon salt and several grinds of pepper. Lightly dredge the chicken in the flour. Brown the chicken on both sides, 1 to 2 minutes per side. Push the chicken to one side of the pan, add the tomato slices, and lightly color them on both sides, 30 seconds to a minute per side. Slide the chicken back into the middle of the pan, and top with the tomato slices. Arrange two mushrooms on top of each piece of chicken.

Scatter the sage leaves into the spaces between the chicken breasts; then add the chopped tomato pieces and wine to the pan. Bring to a boil and reduce until the wine is syrupy, 1 to 2 minutes. Add the chicken broth, and simmer until the chicken is just cooked through and the sauce has thickened slightly, about 5 minutes. Make a space in the pan, and whisk in the remaining 2 tablespoons butter. Sprinkle the cheeses over the chicken pieces. Reduce the heat to low, cover the skillet, and cook until the cheese melts, 5 to 7 minutes.

Uncover, and increase the heat to thicken the sauce slightly. Sprinkle with the parsley, and serve.

Roast Turkey Breast with Dried Fruit and Root Vegetables

Petto di Tacchino Arrosto con Frutta Secca e Tuberi

SERVES 6 TO 8 • You could serve this for a scaled-down Thanksgiving or Friendsgiving when you're not feeding a huge crowd. Or as a weeknight meal, with great leftovers the next day. This is a really good recipe for ensuring a moist turkey breast, since you do not have to deal with the other parts of the turkey and their different cooking times. Just make sure the meat is cooked to 165 degrees.

Active Time: 35 minutes

Total Time: 1 hour 30 minutes

¾ cup dried apricots

¾ cup dried figs

1 cup dry white wine

1 boneless turkey breast (about 2½ pounds), skin on

Kosher salt

Freshly ground black pepper

3 tablespoons extra-virgin olive oil

2 medium turnips, peeled and cut into large chunks (about 12 ounces)

2 large carrots, cut into large chunks

2 parsnips, cut into large chunks

2 medium onions, cut into large chunks

2 sprigs fresh thyme

2 sprigs fresh sage

1 cup chicken stock, preferably homemade or low-sodium store-bought, plus more if needed

Preheat the oven to 400 degrees. Put the fruit in a bowl, pour the wine over it, and let it soak for 10 minutes.

Pat the turkey dry. Season with ½ teaspoon salt and several grinds of pepper. Heat the olive oil in a large, heavy-bottomed roasting pan over medium heat. Add the turkey, skin side down. Brown on both sides, 2 to 3 minutes per side. Push to the side of the roasting pan, and add the turnips, carrots, parsnips, and onions. Season with ½ teaspoon salt and several grinds of pepper. Cook until the vegetables are browned, about 7 minutes.

Push the turkey breast back into the center of the pan, skin side up. Add the thyme and sage sprigs and the dried fruits and the wine in which they were soaked. Increase heat to reduce the wine by half. Add the stock, and bring to a simmer. Cover tightly with foil, and roast in the oven until the internal temperature in the center of the turkey reaches 145 degrees on an instant-read thermometer, 20 to 25 minutes.

Uncover, and roast until the turkey breast is golden and has reached 165 degrees on an instant-read thermometer, about 20 minutes more. Remove the turkey to a cutting board. Let it rest for 10 minutes. Stir the fruits and vegetables and return the pan to the oven until they're nicely caramelized, about 10 minutes more. Discard the herb sprigs.

Thinly slice the turkey against the grain. Serve with the vegetables and fruit, spooning any pan juices over everything.

Skillet Gratinate of Pork, Eggplant, and Zucchini

Filetto di Maiale con Melanzane e Zucchine Gratinati

SERVES 4 • This recipe is similar to the one for Skillet Gratinate of Chicken, Mushrooms, and Tomato (page 140), just with different protein, vegetables, and cheese. Feel free to vary the ingredients to suit what you have on hand—skillet gratinates are one of my favorite one-pot meals, and the possibilities are endless. As with the previous recipe, you can slide this briefly under the broiler if you'd like a browned top.

Active Time: 40 minutes

Total Time: 40 minutes

1 large pork tenderloin (about 1¼ pounds)

Kosher salt

Freshly ground black pepper

2 tablespoons unsalted butter

2 tablespoons extra-virgin olive oil

All-purpose flour, for dredging

1 small Italian eggplant, sliced lengthwise on the bias into 8 slices

1 medium zucchini, sliced lengthwise on the bias into 8 slices

½ cup dry white wine

1½ cups marinara sauce (homemade or store-bought)

8 large fresh basil leaves

8 thin slices mild provolone

¼ cup freshly grated Grana Padano or pecorino

Slice the pork crosswise on the bias into four equal pieces. Butterfly each piece open like a book, attached at the center. Pound each to an even thickness of about ½ inch with a meat mallet. Season with ½ teaspoon salt and several grinds of pepper.

Melt the butter in the olive oil in a large skillet over medium heat. Spread the flour in a shallow bowl or plate. Lightly dredge the pork in the flour. Brown on both sides, 1 to 2 minutes per side. Remove to a plate. Season the eggplant and zucchini with salt and pepper, and brown on both sides, about 2 minutes per side. Remove to the plate with the pork.

Add the wine to the skillet, and increase the heat to reduce the liquid by half. Add the marinara sauce and ½ cup water, and bring it to a simmer. Add the pork back in one layer. Layer two slices of each vegetable on top of the pork cutlets. Top each with two basil leaves, then two slices of provolone, and sprinkle the grated Grana Padano over all. Cover, and simmer until the pork is cooked through and the vegetables are tender, about 10 minutes. Uncover, increase the heat to thicken the sauce slightly, and serve.

Spicy Sheet Pan Pork Chops and Broccoli

Braciole di Maiale Piccanti al Forno con Broccoli

SERVES 4 • This recipe couldn't be simpler, yet it's full of flavor. Pickled peperoncini are the secret ingredient here, adding spice and tanginess in the form of a brine. Peperoncini are also known as Tuscan peppers and are usually sold pickled in glass jars. They are a sweet, mild variety of chili pepper. Usually you see them whole, about 1½ inches long and golden green in color, served alongside Italian antipasto spreads. Preheating the empty sheet pan in the oven is a great way to brown ingredients without having to take the time to sear them on the stove.

Active Time: 20 minutes

Total Time: 50 minutes

Four 10-to-12-ounce pork chops (about 1½ inches thick)

¼ cup extra-virgin olive oil

Kosher salt

1 head broccoli, cut into florets

One 15-ounce can chickpeas, rinsed, drained, and patted dry

8 whole pickled peperoncini, halved lengthwise, plus ¼ cup brine

Preheat the oven to 425 degrees with a rimmed sheet pan on the bottom rack. Rub the pork chops with 2 tablespoons of the olive oil, and season with ½ teaspoon salt. Set the pork chops on the preheated baking sheet, and roast until they're browned on the underside, about 10 minutes.

Meanwhile, toss the broccoli, chickpeas, and peperoncini with the remaining 2 tablespoons olive oil in a large bowl. Season with salt. Flip the pork chops, and set them to one side of the pan. Add the broccoli mixture, peperoncini brine, and ½ cup water. Continue to roast, stirring once halfway through, until the broccoli is charred and tender and the pork chops are cooked through, 25 to 30 minutes, and serve.

Skillet Ricotta Mini–Meat Loaves

Mini Polpettoni con Ricotta

SERVES 4 • Individual meat loaves make this family favorite accessible for a weeknight dinner. The meat mixture also makes excellent meatballs. The unusual ingredient here is the ricotta. Italians love their ricotta, and, added to this recipe, it makes the meat loaves tender and moist. With the mushrooms, this is a complete meal, but adding some mashed potatoes would please everyone, I am sure. Or feel free to add other vegetables along with the mushrooms— onion, celery, carrots, zucchini, or even peas.

Active Time: 25 minutes

Total Time: 55 minutes

½ cup fine dry bread crumbs

⅓ cup milk

1 large egg

3 scallions, including green parts, chopped

2 tablespoons chopped fresh Italian parsley

1 cup fresh ricotta

¼ cup freshly grated Grana Padano or pecorino

12 ounces ground beef

12 ounces ground pork

Kosher salt

Pinch of freshly grated nutmeg

All-purpose flour, for dredging

3 tablespoons extra-virgin olive oil

10 ounces white mushrooms, sliced

3 cups marinara sauce (homemade or store-bought)

2 sprigs fresh basil

Preheat the oven to 400 degrees. Put the bread crumbs, milk, egg, scallions, parsley, ricotta, and Grana Padano in a large bowl. Stir until smooth. Add the beef and pork, 1½ teaspoons salt, and the nutmeg. Mix with your hands to combine and form into four 4-inch-long mini–meat loaves.

Spread some flour in a shallow bowl for dredging. Heat a nonstick skillet over medium-high heat. Add the olive oil. Dredge the meat loaves lightly in flour, and add to the skillet. Brown all over, about 5 minutes. Scatter the mushrooms between the meat loaves. Cook and stir until they begin to brown and wilt, about 5 minutes. Pour the marinara over the meat loaves, and add ½ cup water. Press the basil sprigs into the sauce.

Cover, and bake until it's bubbling, about 15 minutes. Uncover, bake until the meat loaves are crusty and cooked through, about 15 minutes more, remove the basil sprigs, and serve.

Cheesy Veal Chops with Cabbage

Costolette di Vitello Farcite di Fontina con Verza

SERVES 4 • Veal chops are something of a luxury item, so you can also make this with large boneless, skinless chicken breasts or pork chops on the bone. Reduce the total cooking time in the oven by about 10 to 15 minutes if using chicken, and increase it by about 15 minutes if using pork chops.

Active Time: 35 minutes

Total Time: 1 hour 15 minutes

4 bone-in veal chops (about 10 ounces each)

2 cups freshly grated Italian fontina

½ cup freshly grated Grana Padano

4 scallions, including green parts, chopped

Kosher salt

Freshly ground black pepper

2 tablespoons extra-virgin olive oil

All-purpose flour, for dredging

2 tablespoons unsalted butter

2 sprigs fresh sage

1 small head savoy cabbage, sliced

½ cup dry white wine

1 cup chicken stock, preferably homemade or low-sodium store-bought

Preheat the oven to 425 degrees. Cut a pocket down to the bone in each chop, and pound with a meat mallet to flatten slightly and even them out. Combine the fontina, Grana Padano, and scallions in a small bowl; remove and reserve about ½ cup for the topping. Separate the remaining cheese mixture into four portions. Compress the portions a little, and stuff them into the pockets in the chops. Seal closed with toothpicks. Season with ½ teaspoon salt and several grinds of pepper.

Heat the olive oil in a heavy-duty roasting pan over medium heat. Spread the flour on a plate. Dredge the chops lightly in flour. Add them to the roasting pan, and brown on both sides, about 3 minutes per side. Remove them to a plate. Add the butter and sage to the pan. Once the sage is sizzling, add the cabbage, and toss to coat it in the oil. Season with ½ teaspoon salt and several grinds of pepper. Let the cabbage wilt for a minute or two; then add the wine. Simmer to reduce the liquid by half. Add the stock, and bring it to a simmer. Nestle the veal chops in the pan. Cover with foil, and bake for 15 minutes. Uncover, and sprinkle with the reserved cheese mixture. Continue to bake until the chops are cooked through and the cabbage is tender, 20 to 25 minutes more, and serve, removing the sage sprigs.

Skillet Sausages with Fennel and Apples

Salsicce in Padella con Finocchio e Mele

SERVES 4 • This dish is a perfect harmony of savory, sweet, and tart. You can mix up the fruit a bit if you like, substituting firm ripe pears or a cup or two of seedless grapes for some of the apples. If you'd like to stretch this dish to feed a larger crowd, you could also add a few handfuls of halved fingerling potatoes along with the onions.

Active Time: 30 minutes

Total Time: 30 minutes

8 links sweet Italian sausage
(about 1½ pounds)

3 tablespoons extra-virgin olive oil

2 fennel bulbs, trimmed and cut into
1 inch wedges, plus ¼ cup chopped
fronds for garnish

Kosher salt

Freshly ground black pepper

2 large shallots, peeled and cut into
1-inch chunks

2 tablespoons cider vinegar

2 tart apples (such as Granny Smith),
cut into 1-inch chunks

Prick the sausages all over with a fork. Heat the oil in a large skillet over medium heat, and add the sausages. Brown them all over, 5 to 6 minutes, and remove them to a plate. Add the fennel. Season with ½ teaspoon salt and several grinds of pepper. Toss to coat the fennel in the oil. Cover, and cook, tossing once or twice, until it begins to soften and caramelize, about 8 minutes.

Add the shallots, cover again, and cook until they're wilted, about 4 minutes. Add back the sausages, and sprinkle with the vinegar. Stir in the apples. Lower the heat to medium low. Cover, and cook for 7 to 8 minutes more, tossing once halfway through, until the apples and fennel are glazed and tender. (Add a splash of water to the pan if it begins to get too dry before everything is tender.) Garnish with the chopped fennel fronds, and serve.

Skillet Sausage and Peppers

Salsicce e Peperoni in Padella

SERVES 4 • Though I use hot sausages here, you can use any kind of fresh Italian-seasoned sausage you prefer. Chicken or turkey sausages would lighten this dish up a bit, but take care not to overcook them: they dry out faster than pork sausages. Leftovers work well in a frittata or as a sandwich filling.

Active Time: 35 minutes

Total Time: 35 minutes

8 links hot Italian sausage (about 1½ pounds)

3 tablespoons extra-virgin olive oil

2 large sweet onions, thickly sliced

1 red bell pepper, thickly sliced

1 yellow bell pepper, thickly sliced

1 orange bell pepper, thickly sliced

6 garlic cloves, crushed and peeled

Kosher salt

1 tablespoon tomato paste

¾ cup dry white wine

¼ cup chopped fresh basil

Prick the sausages all over with a fork. Heat the olive oil in a large skillet over medium-high heat. Brown the sausages all over, 5 to 6 minutes, and remove them to a plate. Add the onions, peppers, and garlic to the skillet; season lightly with salt. Cover, reduce the heat to medium, and cook until the peppers are wilted, about 8 minutes.

Make a space in the pan, and add the tomato paste there. Toast the tomato paste in that spot for a minute; then stir it into the vegetables. Add the white wine, and bring it to a simmer. Add back the sausages, and adjust the heat to a gentle simmer. Simmer, turning the sausages occasionally, until they are cooked through, 8 to 10 minutes. Increase the heat to reduce any juices in the pan and glaze the sausages. Stir in the basil, and serve.

Lamb and Winter Squash Stew

Spezzatino d'Agnello con Zucca

SERVES 6 TO 8 • I like to purchase a whole piece of boneless lamb shoulder and cut it into chunks myself. It takes a few extra minutes, but the result is much more consistent. Meat packaged as "stew" meat in the grocery store is often odds and ends from different cuts, which will cook at different rates in the pot—some pieces will end up tender and others chewy. You could substitute smoked paprika for the regular sweet paprika here if you want a more intense flavor. I like to serve this stew with mashed potatoes or boiled rice tossed with some butter and grated cheese.

Active Time: 30 minutes

Total Time: 1 hour 50 minutes

3 pounds boneless lamb shoulder, trimmed of excess fat and cut into 2-inch chunks

Kosher salt

Freshly ground black pepper

3 tablespoons extra-virgin olive oil

2 medium onions, chopped

2 stalks celery, cut into ½-inch chunks

2 teaspoons sweet paprika

One 28-ounce can whole San Marzano tomatoes, crushed by hand

3 fresh bay leaves

1 teaspoon dried oregano, preferably Sicilian oregano on the branch

1 small butternut squash, peeled and cut into 1-inch chunks

2 tablespoons chopped fresh Italian parsley

Season the lamb with 1 teaspoon salt and several grinds of pepper. Heat a large Dutch oven over medium heat, and add the oil. When the oil is hot, brown the lamb in batches, about 5 minutes each. Remove the pieces to a plate as they brown.

Once all of the lamb is out of the pot, add the onion and celery. Cook until the vegetables begin to wilt, about 5 minutes. Sprinkle with the paprika, and stir to combine. Add the tomatoes, bay leaves, oregano, and 2 cups water. Add the lamb chunks back to the pot, and season with salt and pepper. Bring the liquid to a simmer, cover, and cook until the lamb is almost tender, about 1 hour. Add the squash (and up to 1 cup water to cover it), and cook, uncovered, until the lamb and squash are both tender, about 20 minutes more. Stir in the parsley, remove the bay leaves, and serve.

London Broil with Peppers and Onion

London Broil con Peperoni e Cipolla

SERVES 4 • The inspiration for this dish is steak pizzaiola, with a marinade to keep it juicy. London broil is a great budget cut of steak that is quite tasty. Just make sure you don't overcook it. It's a lean cut, so it's best served medium rare. It does best with a less acidic marinade, and the longer you can marinate it the better (though it will benefit from even 30 minutes).

Active Time: 30 minutes

Total Time: 1 hour
(includes marinating time)

½ cup red wine

¼ cup drained oil-packed sundried tomatoes

¼ cup loosely packed fresh basil leaves

3 garlic cloves, crushed and peeled

¼ cup plus 2 tablespoons extra-virgin olive oil

One 1½-pound boneless top-round London broil

Kosher salt

1 red bell pepper, cut into thick rings

1 orange bell pepper, cut into thick rings

1 large onion, thickly sliced

Peperoncino flakes

Combine the wine, sundried tomatoes, basil, and garlic in the work bowl of a mini–food processor, and pulse to make a chunky paste. With the machine running, add ¼ cup olive oil to make a smooth paste. Place the London broil flat in a baking dish, and pour the marinade over it. Turn to coat the steak in the marinade. Let it marinate at room temperature for 30 minutes, or longer in the refrigerator if you have time.

Preheat the broiler to high. Remove the steak from the marinade, and season it with salt. Place it on a rimmed baking sheet. Broil until it's well charred on top, 5 to 6 minutes. Turn, and broil until it's charred on the bottom and the internal temperature of the steak reads 125 degrees for medium rare, 3 to 6 minutes, depending on your broiler and the thickness of the steak. Remove the steak to a cutting board to rest.

Carefully toss the peppers and onion on the hot baking sheet with the remaining 2 tablespoons olive oil to coat them in the leftover marinade. Season with salt and peperoncino. Broil until everything is charred on top, about 2 minutes. Toss, and continue to broil until the vegetables are caramelized but still crisp-tender, 2 to 4 minutes more, depending on your broiler. Thinly slice the steak against the grain, and serve with the vegetables.

Mozzarella Cheeseburgers

Cheeseburgers con Mozzarella

SERVES 4 • Everybody loves a good burger, and I am no different, but here I bring the hamburger a bit closer to Italy. Warming the tomatoes for a minute or two brings out their juices and eliminates the need for condiments. I like grating vegetables, like the onion in this recipe, into my burger mixture—it adds flavor and moisture. Try this with beef burgers, as I do here, but it's an even better tip for turkey or chicken burgers, which tend to be dry.

I like to serve my burgers with a simple tossed salad.

Active Time: 30 minutes

Total Time: 30 minutes

1½ pounds ground beef
(80/20 fat content)

½ medium onion, grated on the coarse holes of a box grater

2 teaspoons dried oregano, preferably Sicilian oregano on the branch

Kosher salt

Freshly ground black pepper

2 tablespoons extra-virgin olive oil, plus more for brushing

4 squares focaccia, split crosswise to use as buns

1 ripe beefsteak tomato, cut into 4 thick slices

4 thick slices low-moisture mozzarella

Sliced pickled peperoncini, for topping

Combine the beef, onion, and oregano in a large bowl. Season with 1 teaspoon salt and several grinds of black pepper. Form into four patties about 1 inch thick.

Heat a large cast-iron skillet over medium-high heat. Brush with olive oil. Toast the focaccia squares, cut sides down, until lightly toasted, 2 to 3 minutes. Remove them to serving plates. Add the tomato slices to the pan, season with salt and pepper, and lightly brown on both sides, about 1 minute per side. Remove and reserve them to top the burgers.

Add the burgers, and cook until they're charred on the bottom, about 4 minutes. Flip, and continue to cook until they're done to your liking, 4 to 6 minutes more for medium. Remove the skillet from the heat, add the cheese to the burgers, cover the skillet, and let it sit just until the cheese melts, 1 to 2 minutes.

Transfer the burgers to the focaccia, top them with the tomatoes and sliced peperoncini, and serve.

Beer-Braised Beef Short Ribs

Costolette di Manzo Brasate alla Birra

SERVES 6 • The bones in the short ribs add great flavor to this dish; however, you could also make it with big chunks of beef chuck. If you do, reduce the initial cooking time of the meat by about half. The *pestata* of almonds and porcini does double duty here, adding a rich earthiness to the sauce and helping to thicken it without flour. As much as I enjoy Italian wine with my meals, since this recipe contains beer, here I would accompany it with one of the good artisanal beers coming out of Italy.

Active Time: 35 minutes
Total Time: 2 hours 40 minutes

¼ cup dried porcini

1 cup slivered almonds, toasted

3 tablespoons extra-virgin olive oil

4 pounds bone-in beef short ribs

Kosher salt

Freshly ground black pepper

3 large carrots, cut into 1-inch chunks

2 tablespoons tomato paste

1 tablespoon chopped fresh thyme leaves

2 fresh bay leaves

12 ounces dark ale

6 cups chicken stock, preferably homemade or low-sodium store-bought

3 medium onions, cut into 1-inch chunks

1 pound small red potatoes, halved

2 tablespoons chopped fresh Italian parsley

Combine the porcini and almonds in the work bowl of a mini–food processor. Pulse to make an almost smooth *pestata*.

Heat the olive oil in a large Dutch oven over medium heat. Season the short ribs with 1 teaspoon salt and several grinds of pepper. Brown the short ribs all over, removing them to a plate as they brown, about 5 minutes per batch.

Add the carrots, and toss to coat in the oil. Cook the carrots until they begin to brown, 2 to 3 minutes; then make a space in the pan, and add the tomato paste there. Cook and toast the tomato paste in that space until it darkens a shade or two, about 1 minute. Add the thyme and bay leaves, and stir to combine. Add the *pestata*, and stir to toast lightly, 1 to 2 minutes. Add the beer, bring it to a boil, and cook until the beer is reduced by half. Add back the short ribs, and add 4 cups of the chicken stock. Adjust the heat so the liquid is simmering, set the lid ajar, and simmer until the short ribs are almost tender, 1 hour to 1 hour 15 minutes.

Add the remaining 2 cups stock, the onions, and the potatoes. Return to a simmer, and cook until everything is very tender and the sauce is thick and flavorful, 40 to 50 minutes more. Stir in the parsley, remove the bay leaves, and serve.

Chicken Scaloppine in Lemon Caper Sauce with Spinach

Petto di Pollo al Limone e Capperi con Spinaci

SERVES 4 • This recipe can be made with chicken breast, pork loin or tenderloin, veal cutlets, or turkey breast cutlets. Whatever you use, the meat should be pounded to the same ½-inch thickness. Baby spinach is *en vogue* these days, but don't forget about regular, mature spinach, which is what I call for here. It's got a more pronounced flavor and holds up to longer cooking without falling apart.

Active Time: 30 minutes

Total Time: 30 minutes

1½ pounds boneless, skinless chicken breast (2 or 3 breasts)

Kosher salt

All-purpose flour, for dredging

4 tablespoons unsalted butter

1 tablespoon extra-virgin olive oil

3 garlic cloves, thinly sliced

2 bunches mature spinach, washed well and stemmed (about 1½ pounds)

Peperoncino flakes

1 lemon, thinly sliced, seeds removed, plus 2 tablespoons freshly squeezed lemon juice

3 tablespoons drained capers in brine

½ cup dry white wine

1 cup chicken stock, preferably homemade or low-sodium store-bought

2 tablespoons chopped fresh Italian parsley

Cut the chicken breasts into three or four slices each on the bias, against the grain. Use a meat mallet to pound to an even ½-inch thickness. Season the chicken with ½ teaspoon salt. Spread the flour on a plate or shallow bowl.

Heat a large skillet over medium heat, and add 2 tablespoons of the butter and the olive oil. Lightly dredge the chicken in the flour, and add as many pieces to the skillet as will fit in one layer without crowding. Brown the chicken in batches, removing the slices to a plate as they brown, about 3 minutes per batch.

Once all of the chicken is out of the pan, add the sliced garlic, and cook until it's sizzling, about 1 minute.

Scatter in the spinach, and season with ½ teaspoon salt and a pinch of peperoncino. Toss to coat the spinach in the oil. Cover, and cook until it's wilted, 3 to 4 minutes. Remove the spinach to a serving platter, letting the juices drip back into the pan.

Increase the heat to medium high, and add the remaining 2 tablespoons butter to the skillet. When it's melted, add the lemon slices, and cook, turning once, until browned on the edges, about 1 minute. Add the capers. Let them sizzle a minute; then add the white wine and lemon juice. Simmer rapidly to reduce by half. Add the stock, and simmer rapidly until the liquid is slightly thickened and saucy, 1 to 2 minutes. Slide the chicken back into the pan, and heat it through, 1 to 2 minutes. Sprinkle with the parsley, and toss. Serve the chicken and sauce on top of the spinach.

Beef Goulash

Goulash di Manzo

SERVES 8 • Goulash is a favorite in our family, going all the way back to my grandma, and is a good way to cook the tough part of the cow. In Italy when I was growing up, cows were basically for milk and oxen for work. Raising cows for meat, steaks, was not part of the culture. Since we cooked and ate the meat of older animals, slow cooking techniques were commonly used, as in this recipe. It makes a big batch that will keep in the fridge for several days and freezes well. Since you are adding potatoes to the mix, there is no need to prepare an additional starch.

Active Time: 40 minutes
Total Time: 2 hours 40 minutes

2 ounces pancetta, cut into chunks

3 garlic cloves, crushed and peeled

2 tablespoons extra-virgin olive oil

3 pounds boneless beef chuck, trimmed of excess fat and cut into 2-inch chunks

Kosher salt

Freshly ground black pepper

¼ cup tomato paste

2 teaspoons ground cumin

2 teaspoons sweet paprika

¼ teaspoon ground cloves

1 cup dry white wine

4 fresh bay leaves

1½ pounds medium red potatoes, quartered

3 small onions, quartered, left attached at the root end

2 large carrots, cut into 2-inch chunks

Combine the pancetta and garlic in the work bowl of a mini–food processor. Process to make a smooth paste or *pestata*. Heat a large Dutch oven over medium heat. Add the olive oil. When the oil is hot, scrape in the *pestata*. Cook and stir until the fat is rendered, 2 to 3 minutes.

Season the beef with 1 teaspoon salt and several grinds of pepper. Brown the beef on all sides, 5 to 6 minutes. Make a space in the pan, and add the tomato paste there. Cook and stir the tomato paste in that spot until it toasts and darkens a shade or two, about 1 minute. Sprinkle with the cumin, paprika, and cloves, and stir to combine this with the beef. Add the white wine, and simmer until the liquid is reduced by half, about 2 minutes. Add the bay leaves and enough water to cover the meat, about 4 cups, and simmer, covered, until the meat is just beginning to become tender, about 1 hour. As the meat cooks, check it occasionally, and continue to add water so it is just covered.

Add the potatoes, onions, carrots, and enough water so that the vegetables are just covered, about 2 cups. Cover the pot again, and simmer until the meat and vegetables are tender, about 1 hour more. Uncover and increase the heat to reduce the sauce to your liking. Remove and discard the bay leaves before serving.

Pork Guazzetto with Beans

Guazzetto di Maiale con Fagioli

SERVES 6 TO 8 • Country-style ribs are cut from the blade end of the loin, closer to the pork shoulder, so they're meatier than other cuts of rib. I've added canned beans at the end to make this a true one-dish meal, but if you leave out the beans and shred the meat, it would also make a wonderful dressing for pasta or polenta.

Active Time: 35 minutes

Total Time: 2 hours 20 minutes

3 pounds country-style pork ribs

Kosher salt

3 tablespoons extra-virgin olive oil

1 large onion, cut into large chunks

2 stalks celery, cut into 1-inch chunks

2 large carrots, cut into 1-inch chunks

2 teaspoons chopped fresh thyme leaves

1½ cups dry white wine

Two 28-ounce cans whole San Marzano tomatoes, crushed by hand

4 fresh bay leaves

½ teaspoon peperoncino flakes

Two 15-ounce cans cannellini beans, rinsed and drained

¼ cup chopped fresh Italian parsley

Season the pork ribs all over with 1 teaspoon salt. Heat the olive oil in a large Dutch oven over medium-high heat. Brown the ribs in batches, removing them to a plate as they are browned, about 5 minutes per batch.

Once all of the ribs are out of the pot, add the onion, celery, and carrots, and lower the heat to medium. Cook until the vegetables begin to wilt, 5 to 6 minutes. Sprinkle with the thyme, and stir it in. Add the white wine, and increase the heat to reduce the liquid by half, about 3 minutes. Add the tomatoes and 2 cups water. Add the bay leaves and peperoncino, and season with ½ teaspoon salt. Bring to a simmer, and cook until the ribs are tender, about 1½ hours. Add the beans, and simmer until they absorb some of the sauce and the guazzetto is thick, about 15 minutes. Season with salt. Stir in the parsley, remove the bay leaves, and serve.

Balsamic Chicken Stir-Fry

Bocconcini di Pollo in Padella al Balsamico con Broccoli

SERVES 4 • I love this recipe because it takes the classic stir-fry technique and gives it an Italian twist. The vinegar and honey create a sweet-and-sour glaze for the chicken that everyone will enjoy. In fact, when I was testing this recipe in my kitchen at home, two of my grandchildren, Olivia and Ethan, were visiting, and this was their favorite dish of the day—they both asked for the recipe so they could re-create it at home.

Active Time: 30 minutes
Total Time: 30 minutes

½ cup chicken stock

2 tablespoons balsamic vinegar

1 tablespoon honey

2 teaspoons cornstarch

Kosher salt

3 tablespoons extra-virgin olive oil

1¼ pounds boneless, skinless chicken breasts, cut into thin strips

2 heads broccoli, cut into small florets, stems trimmed and peeled and cut into matchsticks

8 white or cremini mushrooms, trimmed and quartered

1 red bell pepper, cut into thick strips

1 bunch scallions, including green parts, cut into 1-inch pieces

Peperoncino flakes

Cooked rice, for serving, if desired

In a small bowl, stir together the chicken stock, balsamic vinegar, honey, and cornstarch. Season with ½ teaspoon salt, and set aside.

Heat a large nonstick skillet over high heat. Add 1 tablespoon olive oil. Add half of the chicken strips, season with salt, and cook, tossing occasionally, until cooked through and browned all over, about 2 minutes. Remove to a plate, and repeat with the remaining chicken.

When all of the chicken is out of the pan, wipe the skillet clean with a paper towel. Add the remaining 2 tablespoons olive oil over high heat. Add the broccoli, mushrooms, and bell pepper. Toss to coat in the oil. Cook and toss until the vegetables begin to wilt, 3 to 4 minutes. Add the scallions, and a big pinch of peperoncino. Cover, and cook until the vegetables are crisp-tender, 2 to 3 minutes. Uncover, and add the reserved sauce mixture and chicken strips. Cook and toss until the sauce boils and is thickened and the chicken is heated through, 1 to 2 minutes. Serve immediately, ideally with some boiled rice.

DESSERTS

Honeydew Granita 164
Granita di Melone

Grape and Ricotta Pizza 165
Pizza con Ricotta ed Uva

Red Wine Poached Pears 166
Pere in Camicia al Vino Rosso

Mixed Berry Bread Pudding 168
Budino di Pane con Frutti di Bosco

One-Bowl Olive Oil Cake 169
Torta all'Olio d'Oliva

Baked Peaches 170
Pesche al Forno

Apple Cranberry Crumble 171
Crumble di Mele e Mirtilli

Chocolate Chip Ricotta Cookies 173
Biscotti di Ricotta con Gocce di Cioccolato

Quick Strawberry "Shortcake" 174
Shortcake di Fragole

Cheese Plate with Plum Mostarda 175
Formaggi Assortiti con Mostarda di Prugne

In general, Italians are not rich-desserts-after-dinner eaters, and I am no exception. A bowl of seasonal fruits is what you will get at most family tables. Nonetheless, Italy can boast one of the largest dessert, cookie, and ice cream repertoires anywhere. Since this is a book about single pot, pan, and bowl cooking, here are some delicious but easy recipes for dishes that, like all Italian desserts, are never too sweet.

I particularly love fruit desserts, so many of the recipes here include fruit. But there is also a Chocolate Chip Ricotta Cookie (page 173), an all-American favorite that I have given an Italian touch by adding ricotta. The ricotta makes it soft and smooth but still keeps the familiar flavor profile. Of course, I also had to include a simple Italian cake, One-Bowl Olive Oil Cake (page 169), which is excellent both with coffee in the morning and as a quick but rich conclusion to any meal, with the addition of some zabaglione or whipped cream and fresh or poached fruit to top it off. Italians also love to finish their meal with a cheese plate, with a bit of fresh fruit or complex fruit mostardas (Cheese Plate with Plum Mostarda, page 175), which makes for a great ending.

Honeydew Granita

Granita di Melone

SERVES 4 TO 6 • I love the pale-green color of this honeydew granita, but you can make it with any melon you like. It is a very refreshing summer dessert that can be turned into a cocktail by scooping some into a wineglass and adding chilled prosecco.

Active Time: 20 minutes
Total Time: 4 hours 20 minutes

¾ cup sugar
Peel of 1 lime, removed with vegetable peeler
1 cup loosely packed mint sprigs
4 cups cubed ripe honeydew melon
Juice of 4 limes (about ⅓ cup)

Combine the sugar, ¾ cup water, and the lime peel in a small saucepan over medium heat. Cook until the mixture simmers and the sugar has dissolved. Remove from the heat, stir in the mint, and let it cool completely. Remove the lime peel and mint and discard.

Combine the sugar syrup, honeydew, and lime juice in a blender, and purée until very smooth. Pour into a 9-by-13-inch or similar-sized metal pan.

Freeze until ice crystals develop around the edges of the pan, about 45 minutes. Scrape the crystals with a fork to the center of the pan, keeping the granita fluffy. Return it to the freezer, and continue to scrape and freeze every 30 minutes or so, until all of the mixture has formed fluffy flakes, 3 to 4 hours total. Serve in chilled glasses.

Grape and Ricotta Pizza

Pizza con Ricotta ed Uva

SERVES 6 TO 8 • This sweet pizza can serve many purposes—it could be the dessert to end a casual meal, a breakfast or brunch treat, or an anytime snack. Use any type of grapes you like, as long as they are seedless. Halved pitted cherries would also be delicious.

Active Time: 15 minutes

Total Time: 35 minutes

Extra-virgin olive oil, for stretching the dough

1 pound Pizza Dough, purchased or homemade (page 99)

¾ cup seedless red grapes, halved if large

1 tablespoon unsalted butter, melted

1 teaspoon chopped fresh rosemary

¾ cup fresh ricotta

Turbinado sugar, for sprinkling

Preheat the oven to 475 degrees with a rack on the bottom. Lightly oil a quarter-sheet pan. Coat the dough in the oil, and stretch it to the edges of the pan. (If the dough doesn't want to stretch, let it rest for 5 minutes and come back to it and try again.)

Toss the grapes, butter, and rosemary together in a small bowl. Distribute the ricotta in dollops all over the pizza. Add the grapes in the spaces between the ricotta dollops. Sprinkle with the turbinado sugar. Bake on the bottom rack until the crust is crisp and golden and the grapes are juicy, 20 to 22 minutes, and serve.

Red Wine Poached Pears

Pere in Camicia al Vino Rosso

SERVES 4 • These are delicious on their own, but a crisp cookie is a lovely accompaniment. If you have any pears left over, you can refrigerate them in their syrup. Slice them and use as a crêpe filling or as a topping for a plain cake, like my One-Bowl Olive Oil Cake (page 169). These pears will keep (and only get better and deeper in color!) in the refrigerator in their syrup for up to a week.

Active Time: 10 minutes

Total Time: 1 hour 10 minutes

4 medium-sized ripe Bosc pears

1 orange

3 cups red wine

1 cup sugar

1 cinnamon stick

1 teaspoon allspice berries

2 whole cloves

Peel the pears; then halve and core them. Put the pear halves in a large saucepan. Remove the peel (without the pith) from the orange, and add it to the pot. Juice the orange into the pot. Add the red wine, sugar, cinnamon stick, allspice, cloves, and enough water to cover the pears, 2 to 3 cups.

Bring the liquid to a simmer. Simmer very gently until the pears are tender all the way through, about 15 minutes. Let them cool in the syrup for about 30 minutes; then remove them to a serving dish. Simmer the remaining liquid to reduce it to about 2 cups syrup, about 15 minutes. Strain the syrup over the pears, and let cool slightly.

Serve the pears drizzled with the warm syrup.

Mixed Berry Bread Pudding

Budino di Pane con Frutti di Bosco

SERVES 8 • This recipe is the definition of flexibility—use any day-old, neutral-tasting bread you have, whether it's an eggy bread like brioche or a simple white country bread. (If the crusts are very tough, remove them.) You could even take this to the next level and use day-old croissants. Berries are wonderful here, but you can also use chopped peaches or plums, or leave out the fresh fruit entirely and add a handful or two of dried fruit or chocolate chips.

Active Time: 15 minutes

Total Time: 2 hours
(includes cooling time)

1 tablespoon unsalted butter, at room temperature

¾ cup sugar, plus more for the baking dish and sprinkling

4 large eggs

Kosher salt

2 cups half-and-half (or 1 cup milk, 1 cup cream)

1 teaspoon pure vanilla extract

½ teaspoon almond extract

8 cups cubed day-old brioche or country bread (about 16 ounces)

1½ cups mixed berries (blueberries, raspberries, and/or blackberries)

¼ cup sliced almonds

Preheat the oven to 350 degrees.

Coat a 9-by-13-inch baking dish with the butter, and sprinkle with sugar to coat. Beat the eggs, ¾ cup sugar, and ¼ teaspoon salt in a large bowl until smooth. Whisk in the half-and-half, vanilla, and almond extract until smooth. Add the bread cubes, and press them down to submerge. Let the bread soak in the custard for 15 minutes.

Bring a kettle of water to a boil. Pour the bread and custard into the prepared baking dish. Sprinkle with the berries. Sprinkle the almonds over the berries, and top with a dusting of sugar.

Set the baking dish in a roasting pan, and pour in boiling water to come halfway up the sides of the baking dish. Bake until the top is puffed and the bread pudding is just set, about 1 hour. It should still be slightly jiggly in the center. Remove from the oven, and let it cool for 30 minutes in the roasting pan. Serve warm or at room temperature.

One-Bowl Olive Oil Cake

Torta all'Olio d'Oliva

SERVES 8 • Though it's delicious on its own, this simple cake can be dressed up in any number of ways, making it one of the most versatile dessert recipes you'll have in your recipe box. Poached or sautéed fresh fruit makes a lovely topping—or try it as I like it best, with a spoonful of preserved Amarena cherries in syrup (Fabbri makes a good product) and a dollop of whipped cream. The limoncello adds an authentic Italian touch here, but you could substitute brandy or another liqueur—or even freshly squeezed lemon juice. This cake keeps well, and is even moister after a day or two.

Active Time: 10 minutes

Total Time: 1 hour 15 minutes
(includes cooling time)

½ cup extra-virgin olive oil, plus more for the pan

1½ cups all-purpose flour, plus more for the pan

1 cup sugar

1 teaspoon freshly grated lemon zest

2 large eggs, plus 1 yolk

½ cup milk

2 tablespoons limoncello

2 teaspoons pure vanilla extract

1½ teaspoons baking powder

Kosher salt

Preheat the oven to 350 degrees. Brush an 8-inch round cake pan with olive oil, and dust it with flour, tapping out the excess. Line the bottom with a round of parchment.

Whisk the ½ cup olive oil, sugar, lemon zest, eggs, and yolk in a large bowl until the mixture is light, about 1 minute. Whisk in the milk, limoncello, and vanilla until smooth. Add the 1½ cups flour, baking powder, and ¼ teaspoon salt, and whisk just until smooth.

Pour the batter into the prepared pan, and bake until a tester inserted in the center comes out clean, 30 to 35 minutes. Cool in the pan on a rack for 15 minutes; then unmold and cool completely before serving.

Baked Peaches

Pesche al Forno

SERVES 6 • You can make this with any stone fruit you like—plums and apricots also work, though the baking time may be a bit shorter. Make sure the peaches are ripe but still firm. I like to serve these peaches warm with a scoop of vanilla ice cream, and they also make a wonderful breakfast the next day, topped with plain yogurt and a little granola.

Active Time: 10 minutes

Total Time: 50 minutes

6 medium peaches

4 tablespoons unsalted butter, melted

½ cup peach or apricot preserves

2 tablespoons freshly squeezed lemon juice

1 vanilla bean, halved lengthwise

¼ cup light-brown sugar

Preheat the oven to 400 degrees. Halve the peaches and remove the pits. Put them, cut side up, in a 9-by-13-inch baking dish.

Combine the melted butter, preserves, and lemon juice in a small bowl. Scrape the seeds from the vanilla bean into the bowl, and stir. Spoon the mixture over the peaches. Sprinkle the peaches with the brown sugar. Pour ½ cup water into the baking pan, and cover with foil. Bake until the peaches are just beginning to become tender, about 20 minutes.

Uncover, baste the peaches with their juices, and increase the oven temperature to 425 degrees. Bake until the peaches are tender and caramelized, 20 to 30 minutes more, depending on their size and ripeness, and serve.

Apple Cranberry Crumble

Crumble di Mele e Mirtilli

SERVES 6 TO 8 • Crumbles are not Italian, but I have learned to love them because they are very Italian in spirit—fresh fruit and a simple topping come together to create a homey dessert everyone will love. The trick to making a crisp, clumpy topping is to squeeze the clumps a little.

Active Time: 20 minutes

Total Time: 1 hour 15 minutes

Filling

2 tablespoons unsalted butter, cold, cut into pieces, plus 1 tablespoon, softened, for the skillet

3 pounds cooking apples, such as Golden Delicious, peeled and cut into chunks

2 cups fresh cranberries

½ cup granulated sugar

2 tablespoons all-purpose flour

Kosher salt

1 tablespoon freshly squeezed lemon juice

Topping

¾ cup all-purpose flour

¾ cup chopped almonds

¾ cup rolled oats (old-fashioned, not instant)

¾ cup packed light-brown sugar

½ teaspoon ground ginger

¼ teaspoon freshly grated nutmeg

Kosher salt

1 stick unsalted butter, slightly softened

Preheat the oven to 350 degrees. Butter a large cast-iron skillet. Combine the apples, cranberries, granulated sugar, flour, ¼ teaspoon salt, and lemon juice in a large bowl, and toss well. Transfer to the skillet. Dot the top with the cold butter pieces.

Wipe out the bowl, and make the topping. Add the flour, almonds, oats, brown sugar, ginger, nutmeg, and ¼ teaspoon salt to the bowl. Toss to combine. Cut the butter into five or six pieces. Work the butter in with your fingers until the topping is evenly moistened.

Squeeze clumps of the topping in your palm, a few tablespoons at a time, and scatter them over the fruit. Bake until the crumble topping is golden and crisp and the fruit juices are bubbly, 40 to 50 minutes. Cool on a rack, and serve warm or at room temperature.

Chocolate Chip Ricotta Cookies

Biscotti di Ricotta con Gocce di Cioccolato

MAKES ABOUT 2½ DOZEN • I've been making ricotta cookies for years, and my family has always loved these simple, cakey, one-bowl treats. Adding chocolate chips makes them even better! Use a good-quality fresh ricotta here—you will taste the difference.

Active Time: 15 minutes

Total Time: 55 minutes

1 stick unsalted butter, at room temperature

1 cup granulated sugar

2 large eggs

8 ounces fresh ricotta

1 teaspoon pure vanilla extract

2½ cups all-purpose flour

2 teaspoons baking powder

Kosher salt

1 cup mini–chocolate chips

Confectioners' sugar, for dusting, if desired

Preheat the oven to 350 degrees. Line two baking sheets with parchment.

Cream the butter and granulated sugar in a large bowl with a handheld mixer on high speed until light and fluffy, about 2 minutes. Reduce the speed to medium, and add the eggs. Beat until smooth. Add the ricotta and vanilla, and beat to combine.

Sift the flour and baking powder right into the bowl, and add a pinch of salt. Mix on low speed until just combined. Stir in the chocolate chips by hand.

Drop the cookies in heaping tablespoons onto the baking sheets, leaving about 2 inches between cookies, in three rows of five. Bake, rotating the trays from top to bottom halfway through, until the cookies are puffed and golden at the edges, 16 to 18 minutes. Remove to a wire rack to cool.

Dust the cookies with confectioners' sugar before serving, if desired.

Quick Strawberry "Shortcake"

Shortcake di Fragole

SERVES 4 • I am a big fan of *dolci di cucchiaio,* or spoon desserts. They're simple, creamy, and homey, and meant to be eaten with a spoon at the end of a casual meal. This is the quickest example I can think of, for when you want something sweet but don't want to fuss. You can use any bite-sized vanilla-flavored cookie you like here, as long as it's crisp enough to add contrast to the whipped cream and berries. I don't like overly sweet desserts, so I chose to leave the strawberries and whipped cream unsweetened, but you may add a bit of sugar to either, if you prefer.

Active Time: 20 minutes

Total Time: 30 minutes

1 pint ripe strawberries, cored and quartered

2 tablespoons strawberry liqueur (or rum or brandy)

¾ cup heavy cream, chilled

24 bite-sized vanilla wafer cookies (such as Loacker) or other very small crisp vanilla cookies, for serving

Toss the strawberries in a medium bowl with the liqueur, and let macerate for 10 minutes.

Whisk the cream to soft peaks.

To serve, spoon some strawberries into four sundae dishes or wineglasses. Top with a few cookies and some whipped cream. Repeat with more strawberries, cookies, and whipped cream. Top with one final strawberry and cookie, and serve immediately.

Cheese Plate with Plum Mostarda

Formaggi Assortiti con Mostarda di Prugne

MAKES ABOUT 3 CUPS MOSTARDA • A platter of cheese and some fresh fruit is the simplest way to end a good meal. Take it a step further with a store-bought or homemade mostarda. This makes about 3 cups, which is enough for quite a few cheese plates, but it will keep well in the refrigerator for a few weeks or more. This mostarda also makes a good sandwich spread or condiment for pork or chicken.

When assembling a cheese plate, keep it simple—three cheeses, or four at the most. A good rule is to choose one made from each type of milk—cow, goat, and sheep. Try to vary the pungency: if you have a very earthy or pungent cheese, also offer something mild and something in the middle. Finally, vary the textures—if you've got a grainy and crumbly cheese, like Grana Padano or pecorino (two of my favorites), offer one that's semi-hard and more sliceable and one that's creamy and spreadable. Plan on buying an ounce or so of each cheese per person. Add some seasonal fresh fruit, some nuts, and your mostarda, and you're all set!

Active Time: 20 minutes

Total Time: 30 minutes

Plum Mostarda

½ cup white wine

½ cup red wine vinegar

2 tablespoons dry mustard

3 pounds mixed plums, pitted and cut into ½-inch chunks

¾ cup sugar

1 tablespoon grated fresh ginger

2 teaspoons yellow mustard seeds

2 teaspoons kosher salt

¼ teaspoon peperoncino flakes

Combine the white wine and vinegar in a large saucepan, whisk in the dry mustard until smooth, and bring to a simmer. Add the plums, sugar, ginger, mustard seeds, salt, and peperoncino, and continue to bring to a simmer over medium-low heat. Cook, stirring often (especially toward the end, as it thickens), until thick and syrupy, about 15 minutes. Cool, and pack into a lidded jar. The mostarda will keep 3 to 4 weeks in the refrigerator.

My Kitchen Tools

These are the essential items I have in my kitchen and find myself reaching for over and over again. When you are cooking with just one or two pots or pans, you want to make sure you can rely on them. Some of the tools in my kitchen are older than my grandchildren! If you invest in a quality item and take care of it, it will last for a very long time.

Pots and Pans

Pasta/stock pot: A large (8 to 10 quarts) stainless steel pot—no pasta insert needed!

Roasting pan with rack: Look for one with a heavy bottom so that you can also brown the meat right in the pan.

Large enameled cast-iron Dutch oven: I find an 8- or 9-quart size the best for large braises and batches of soup.

Large, low-sided enameled cast-iron pan or large straight-sided skillet: For making risottos.

Large stainless steel pot: About 6 quarts, ideal for smaller batches of soup or boiling vegetables.

Medium saucepan: A 2-quart capacity is perfect.

Small saucepan: I prefer one with a heavy bottom and an oven-safe handle.

Large and medium stainless steel skillets: A heavy bottom and an oven-safe handle are important.

Large and medium nonstick skillets: As when choosing a saucepan and a skillet, I look for one with a heavy bottom and an oven-safe handle.

Large cast-iron skillet: My favorite pan in the kitchen for my grandma's Skillet Chicken Thighs with Cerignola Olives and Potatoes (page 135) and other stovetop meals.

Several rimmed, heavy-duty half-sheet pans.

9-by-13-inch baking dish, glass or ceramic.

8-by-8-inch baking dish, glass or ceramic.

Tools

Large, thick wooden cutting board.

Sharp knives: Invest in a good set—a chef's knife, a paring knife, a medium-sized utility knife, and a serrated knife are the basics to start with.

Wooden spoons.

Locking metal tongs.

Large colander.

Large spider.

Medium ladle.

Tasting spoons: I keep a small crock of them handy as I cook, because tasting as you go is so important.

Box grater.

Microplane grater.

Sharp vegetable peeler: The key word here is "sharp"—they're inexpensive, so replace them as they begin to dull.

Sturdy whisk.

Mandoline: Not essential, but helpful. The smaller plastic ones are less expensive and work very well.

Rubber spatulas.

Wet and dry measuring cups: They are not interchangeable, especially for baking, so invest in a full set of each.

Peppermill.

Mise en place bowls: Having all of your ingredients prepped and ready to go will help you spend less time at the stove. A set or two of nested bowls will help you prep and stay organized.

Potato masher and potato ricer: Do you really need both? I do—I like the masher for coarse vegetable purées and use the ricer to mash smooth potatoes for gnocchi, and also for squeezing out excess liquid from cooked vegetables, like spinach.

Salad spinner.

Kitchen shears.

Freezer-safe containers for leftovers: The most in-demand items in my kitchen. I keep both pint and quart sizes on hand. I always make big batches and package up leftovers—whether it is for a friend in need or a quick meal in my own kitchen, leftovers are the best!

Metal slotted fish spatula.

Nonstick spatula.

Large slotted and plain metal spoons.

Meat mallet.

Oil thermometer: Not essential, but takes the guesswork out of frying.

Meat thermometer.

Appliances

Food processor.

Mini–food processor: Perhaps not essential, but I find it more efficient to make smaller batches of condiments like pesto and flavored oils in one of these.

Blender and immersion blender.

Stand mixer with whisk, paddle, and dough hook attachments.

Electric juicer: Again, not essential, but I have one and find it speedy and convenient.

Spice/coffee grinder.

Index

(Page references in *italics* refer to illustrations.)

Lidia Bastianich, Emmy Award–winning public-television host, best-selling cookbook author, restaurateur, and owner of a flourishing food-and-entertainment business, has married her two passions in life—her family and food—to create multiple culinary endeavors.

Lidia's cookbooks, coauthored with her daughter, Tanya, include *Lidia's Celebrate Like an Italian*, *Lidia's Commonsense Italian Cooking*, *Lidia's Favorite Recipes*, *Lidia's Italy in America*, *Lidia Cooks from the Heart of Italy*, and *Lidia's Italy*—all companion books to the Emmy-winning and three-time-nominated television series *Lidia's Kitchen*, *Lidia's Italy in America*, and *Lidia's Italy*, which have aired internationally, in Mexico, Canada, the Middle East, Croatia, and the U.K. Lidia has also published *Felidia*, *Lidia's Mastering the Art of Italian Cuisine*, *Lidia's Family Table*, *Lidia's Italian-American Kitchen*, *Lidia's Italian Table*, and *La Cucina di Lidia*, and three children's books: *Nonna Tell Me a Story: Lidia's Christmas Kitchen*, *Lidia's Family Kitchen: Nonna's Birthday Surprise*, and *Lidia's Egg-citing Farm Adventure*, as well as a memoir, *My American Dream*. Lidia is the chef-owner, with her son, Joseph, of Becco. She is also the founder of Tavola Productions, an entertainment company that produces high-quality broadcast productions. Lidia also has a line of dry pastas and all-natural sauces, called LIDIA'S organic pasta sauces. Along with her son, Joe Bastianich, and Oscar Farinetti, she opened Eataly, the largest artisanal Italian food-and-wine marketplaces in New York City, Chicago, Boston, Los Angeles, Las Vegas, and São Paulo, Brazil.

Tanya Bastianich Manuali's visits to Italy as a child sparked her passion for the country's art and culture. She dedicated herself to the study of Italian Renaissance art during her college years at Georgetown; she then earned a master's degree from Syracuse University and a doctorate from Oxford University. She lived and studied in many regions of Italy for several years, and taught art history to American students in Florence. But it was in New York that she met her husband, Corrado Manuali, who came from Rome.

Tanya is integrally involved in the production of Lidia's public-television series, as an owner and executive producer of Tavola Productions, and is active in the family restaurant business. In 2019, Tanya joined her brother in operating several other restaurants, including Babbo, Lupa, Pizzeria Mozza, Osteria Mozza, and Chi Spacca. Tanya owns Lidia's in Kansas City. She has also led the development of the website lidiasitaly.com, and the related publications and merchandise lines of tableware and cookware. Tanya is a member of Les Dames d'Escoffier (New York chapter), a philanthropic organization of women leaders in the fields of food, fine beverages, and hospitality.

Together with Corrado, Tanya oversees the production and expansion of the LIDIA'S food line of all-natural pastas and sauces. Tanya has coauthored several books with her mother, including *Felidia, Lidia's Celebrate Like an Italian, Lidia's Mastering the Art of Italian Cuisine, Lidia's Commonsense Italian Cooking, Lidia's Favorite Recipes, Lidia's Italy, Lidia Cooks from the Heart of Italy*, and *Lidia's Italy in America*. In 2010, Tanya coauthored *Reflections of the Breast: Breast Cancer in Art Through the Ages*, a social–art-historical look at breast cancer in art from ancient Egypt to today. In 2014, Tanya wrote *Healthy Pasta* with her brother, Joe. Tanya and Corrado live in New York City with their children, Lorenzo and Julia.

A NOTE ON THE TYPE

This book was set in Janson, a typeface long thought to have been made by the Dutchman Anton Janson, who was a practicing typefounder in Leipzig during the years 1668–1687. However, it has been conclusively demonstrated that these types are actually the work of Nicholas Kis (1650–1702), a Hungarian, who most probably learned his trade from the master Dutch typefounder Dirk Voskens. The type is an excellent example of the influential and sturdy Dutch types that prevailed in England up to the time William Caslon (1692–1766) developed his own incomparable designs from them.

Composed by North Market Street Graphics, Lancaster, Pennsylvania

Printed and bound by Friesens, Altona, Manitoba

Designed by Anna B. Knighton